AF540518

HUMAN DEVELOPMENT

About the Editor

Keya Sengupta is presently a Professor at Indian Institute of Management, Shillong and was formerly the Dean, School of Social Sciences and also the Head, Department of Economics at Assam Central University. Prof. Sengupta is engaged in teaching of Economics and research for over thirty years. She has authored and also edited many books and published many research papers in journals of repute including Artha Vijnana, Man and Development, Finance India, Agricultural Situation in India etc. She has also presented a good number of papers in national and international seminars and delivered lectures in many universities and institutes. Prof Sengupta has also completed major Research Projects of UGC, ICSSR and UNDP and also undertaken Research Consultancy of CII and Planning Commission. Recently, she was selected for the Indo French Social Scientist Exchange Programme and was invited by Foundation Maison des Sciences de l'Hommes Paris, France. She has also visited Belgium, Holland, Germany, Scotland and England in connection with various types of academic work.

HUMAN DEVELOPMENT

Multi Dimensional Approach
to
Human Well-Being

Edited by
KEYA SENGUPTA

CONCEPT PUBLISHING COMPANY PVT. LTD.,
NEW DELHI-110059

ISBN-13-978-81-8069-683-1

First Published 2010

Published and Printed by

Concept Publishing Company Pvt. Ltd.
Regd. Office:
A/15-16, Commercial Block, Mohan Garden
New Delhi-110059 (India)
Phones : 25351460, 25351794, *Fax* : 091-11-25357109
Email : publishing@conceptpub.com
Website: www.conceptpub.com

Editorial Office:
H-13, Bali Nagar, New Delhi-110 015, India.

Cataloging in Publication Data-- *Courtesy:* D.K. Agencies (P) Ltd. <docinfo@dkagencies.com>

Human development : multi dimensional approach to human well-being / edited by Keya Sengupta.
p. cm.
Contributed articles in Indian context.
Includes bibliographical references.
Includes index.
ISBN 13: 9788180696831 ISBN 10: 818696839

1. Quality of life--India. 2. Economic development--India. 3. Regional planning--India. 4. Education--India. 5. Social values--India. I. Sengupta, Keya, 1955-

DDC 307.140954 22

Dedicated to
Baba and Ma

Preface

Human development has now being accepted as the new paradigm to evaluate the well-being of people of all places. It is not only confined to economic well-being alone but encompasses a wide range of factors that contribute in enhancing human welfare. This holistic idea of well-being is extremely crucial because well-being cannot be determined by just one or two factors. High income alone cannot raise well-being without possessing good health, just as good health and education without human value is meaningless. Pollution free environment plays a pivotal role in sustaining human development, absence of which may not only jeopardize health and life but may also impede economic development and growth, which in turn may seriously hamper achieving the objectives of human development. Human welfare may become a total farce in the absence of human rights which has over the years been severely violated due to wars, aggression and army rules. Democracies during most of these times are better equipped to meet the social needs of the common people and in raising human development in general. Striving to achieve all these goals may not be possible without good governance. For attaining all these objectives, it is essential to first identify the various problems that brings down human development. Secondly, the identified problems need to be analysed and examined as how they may reverse the path of human development. In the process, they also provide solution to every nation as how best they can view human development as a holistic development goal. The goals, however, can be attained and the appropriate strategies adopted only in the right political perspective. It is, therefore, pertinent that attaining the broader goals of human development through the right balancing of policies in every direction of human well-being requires a strong political will. Strong political will in turn necessitates transparent and accountable governance. It is, therefore, crucial that human development in its true sense can be attained only when there is the right blending of democratic governance and economic development as well as socio-economic development. Inadequate attention to all these diverse aspects of human development may trigger off unrest and revolt by the common man, which in turn may make achieving the targets of long term development extremely difficult.

In an attempt to capture all these varied aspects of human well-being, the book presents diverse views of experts and specialists in various areas of human development. The book will be a useful reading for all those working in the area of human development and welfare.

Keya Sengupta
Editor

Acknowledgement

I express my sincere gratitude and thanks to all those who have contributed their valuable research papers in bringing out this book. Each one of the author has tried to examine human development from the perspective of their own discipline so that the book has for the first time emerged as the product of research work with a holistic approach to human development.

Keya Sengupta

Editorial Note

Human Development today is an important tool for examining the living standards and well-being of people all over the world. Well-being of man is not evaluated any more in terms of economic factors alone, but is accepted as a holistic concept which incorporates his cultural, social, political, along with economic well-being, as well as all other factors that go to make life more meaningful and worth living. In view of this kind of an interdisciplinary approach to evaluate the condition of living of the common man, the present book contains fourteen well researched papers from a wide and diverse perspective written by well known scholars in this field, taking almost every aspect of human well-being into consideration. The book has been divided into five sections. Each section attempts to view and analyse the issues of Human Development from its own discipline.

The first section of the book is entitled, *Significance of Human Development*. In this section, Keya Sengupta in her paper entitled, "Significance and Relevance of the Study of Human Development", has highlighted, the meaning of Human Development and the importance of the study of Human Development, both from the theoretical as well as practical point of view.

The second section on *Human Development and Economic Development* contains four papers. All these papers have examined the issues of Human Development from the point of view of various economic indicators of Human Development. The first paper is by Pulin B. Nayak entitled "Human Development and the Indian Context'. In this paper he highlights the commendable performance of the Indian Economy as revealed by the various economic indicators. However, he also focuses attention to the fact that the same is not matched by the performance in the social sector. There is wide sectoral, regional and social disparity in the Indian economy, due to which wide gap between the performance of the economic and social sector is evident. Sibranjan Misra in his paper 'Towards a Human Development Strategy" maintains that per capita income is undoubtedly an important determinant of Human Development but even more important is the public money which determines public expenditure in the social sector. This according to him becomes necessary due to market failures. However, in the Indian Context, even social sector spending is lopsided due to which, there is also a great deal of lopsidedness even in the level of Human Development in India. In the next paper "Sustainable Human Development and Accelerating Economic Growth", P.K. Chaubey maintains that Human Development without economic growth is unattainable. But accelerating growth rate may make economic growth rate and human development unsustainable in the long run if attention is not drawn to environmental sustainability. Environmental sustainability in turn will also ensure inter-generational sustainability of Human Development. Raj Kumar Sen in his paper on "Climate Change and Human Development: HDR 2007/2008" talking on similar lines discusses the effect of environmental pollution on Human Development in the light of the Human Development Report of 2007. In this context, he discusses the responsibilities of specially the highly developed countries of the West and the various measures undertaken for the reduction of such wide extent of pollution.

The Third Section deals with the *Regional Dimensions of Economic Development,* containing three papers. The first paper by Niranjan Roy entitled "Inter-District Variations in the Level of Human Development in Assam" discusses the wide inter-district variation in the level of human development in Assam and attempts to identify the reasons for the same. Gender disparity according to him is even wider than the disparity of Human Development in the state. Indraneel Bhowmik in his paper "Human Development among the Workers of Transport sector in Tripura", examines the various indicators of Human Development of different urban passenger modes of transport and concludes that differences in the level of skill and education is a direct determinant of the differences in the quality of life of the transport workers of the state. The next paper in this section is by Tarun Bikash Sukai on "Migration and Development: Implications for Human Development", the discussion of which centres around the economic and political migrants and their level of human development as well as human rights which according to this study is much lower than most other people. The reasons for such problems are also examined in the paper.

The Fourth Section deals with *Human Development in the Context of Human Resource Development* which contains three papers. The first paper is by Prof. Shri Prakash entitled "Human Resource Allocation and Education-Employment Trade-Offs" in which the author within the Input-Output Framework, examines the choice making behaviour of Households. He maintains that there is a vicious circle of low education, low income parent's children have low education and low income, because they cannot afford better education and looks for opportunities to substitute education by low paid jobs. This is unlike the experience of the children of higher educated and better employed parents. In the joint paper on "Education as a Base of Human Development", Manosi Chaudhuri, Varimna Singh and Vishal Agarwal argue that to maintain the current growth rate of the Indian Economy, growth momentum of the tertiary sector which is the fastest growing sector of the Indian Economy has to be maintained. For this it is necessary that the quantity as well as the quality of this sector has to be maintained as well. Poor performance in the various indicators of Human Development as is evident in India, can only pull down the quality of manpower which is so vital during globalisation. The work reveals that there is a wide regional disparity in the indicators of quality education in India. Arup Barman, in his paper on, "Human Resource Development under Competitive Regime" makes an attempt to establish a relationship between Human Development indicators and economic competitive index which is so important during globalisation. According to the study, India suffers from a low competitive edge over other countries mainly because she suffers from low level of Human Development.

Section Five is on *Human Development and Human Values* in which there are three papers. The first paper is by Amiya P. Sen on "Gandhi, Gandhians and Thoughts on Indian Development: Random Reflections on Human Development", in which the author focuses attention to the stark reality of the disparity of income, consumption habits and levels of living in India and wonders whether each one of us has any responsibility towards the less well-off in the society. In this respect, he examines the views of Gandhi and his followers such as Kumarappa. Projit Kumar Palit in his paper on "Human Development and Early Indian Thoughts" examines the idea of human development which has been imbibed since earlier times in terms of human values evident in ancient Indian Thoughts. He compares this with the thoughts of the ancient Greeks. In this connection he also examines the universal Vedantic vision of man as propounded by

Swami Vivekananda. The other paper in this section by Partha Pratim Paul entitled 'Right to Work: A Constitutional Contour and its Human Development Perspective', discusses the need for employment for ensuring Human Development. However, according to him the concept of "right to work" advocated in the Constitution do not guarantee the right of every citizen, which is surely not congenial for attaining human development.

Keya Sengupta
Editor

Contents

List of the Contributors

Amiya P. Sen, Department of History, Director, Centre for Gandhian Study, Jamia Millia Islamia University, New Delhi.

Arup Barman, Department of Business Administration, Assam Central University, Silchar, Assam.

Indraneel Bhowmik, Women's College, Agartala, Tripura.

Keya Sengupta, Professor, Indian Institute of Management, Shillong, Meghalaya.

Manosi Chaudhuri, Assistant Professor, Birla Institute of Management Technology, Greater Noida.

Niranjan Roy, Department of Economics, Assam Central University, Silchar, Assam.

P.K. Choubey, Professor Indian Institute of Public Administration, New Delhi.

Partha Pratim Paul, Department of Law, University of North Bengal, District: Darjeeling (West Bengal).

Projit Kumar Palit, Department of History, Assam Central University, Silchar, Assam.

Pulin B. Nayak, Director, Institute of Economic Growth, New Delhi.

Raj Kumar Sen, Director, Centre for Studies on Environment and Sustainable Development (CSESD), Rabindra Bharati University, Kolkata.

Shri Prakash, Dean, Reseach, Birla Institute of Management Technology, Greater Noida.

Sibranjan Misra, Department of Economics, Viswa Bharati, Shantiniketan, West Bengal.

Tarun Bikash Sukai, Department of Social Work, Assam Central University, Silchar, Assam.

Varimna Singh, Birla Institute of Management Technology, Greater Noida.

Vishal Agarwal, Birla Institute of Management Technology, Greater Noida.

Section One

Significance of Human Development

1

Human Development: The New Approach to Development Strategy

KEYA SENGUPTA

Introduction

Development problems in less developing nations/regions, must be seen in a much broader perspective in comparison to traditional economics of a developed one. Problems of such economies have to be analysed within the context of the overall social system of the area concerned. Social system implies the interdependent relationship between economic and non-economic factors. Among non-economic factors we have attitude towards life, work, legal and administrative structures, patterns of kinship and religion, cultural traditions, system of land tenure, the authority and integrity of government agencies and the degree of people's participation in development decisions and activities and the flexibility or rigidity of economic and social classes. Due to wide variation of these issues from one country to another, and inter as well as intra-regional variations and also differences from one social and cultural setting to another, such studies relating to the problems of one region cannot be imposed on another. Tackling these issues in an attempt at initiating economic development sometime pose greater problem. Raising production level, living standards and the other macro economic indicators of growth are all functions of local history, expectations, values, incentives, attitudes, beliefs and institutional and power structure. Added to these are also important factors like savings, investment, product factor prices, foreign exchange rate etc. Economists sometimes dismiss these important non-economic variables as "non-quantifiable", without realizing that they play a very important role in the success or failure of the development effort (Todaro, 2003).

All these disturbing features have harmed the long-term development of backward regions, and failed to initiate the process of sustained development. Pure economic theory of rationality which may justify extreme inequality of income on grounds of efficiency and marginal productivity theory of distribution, may be a dangerous proposition for such places. What may be rational behaviour from the macro-economic point of view, may not be an ideal condition from the micro-economic point of view.

A humanistic approach of development model based on wage goods paradigm may be a possible alternative. The main focus of attention of these models should be based on the paradigm of human development, in its various dimensions. Various aspects of human well-being such as food, nutrition, shelter, education, health and various other amenities, which constitute a good quality life, should occupy the centre stage of all development efforts. Such objectives carefully researched, studied and analyzed, if integrated into growth models, need not be at the cost of rational economic behaviour and anti-growth. Rational economic approach may not always be helpful in clarifying such problems and unconventional approaches may often have to be adopted to solve what may superficially appear to be conventional economic problems. Though traditional economic approach can play a useful role in improving our understanding of development problems, but they should not act as obstacles to the realities of local conditions in less developed countries. Hence the necessity of ensuring state intervention for synthesizing economic rationality of market forces and welfare of the common man.

Importance and Significance of the Study of Human Development

The essence of all these issues such as education, health and various other factors which determine the conditions of living of the common man are captured in the newly emerged concept of Human Development. The acceptance of this new idea has significantly broadened the narrow conventional development paradigm. The response of the new development economics to the changing realities of life in the developing countries and the new theoretical advances made in mainstream economics has been both positive and negative. This is evident in the greater emphasis on Human Development. This is also evident from the regular publication of the Human Development Report by UNDP, since 1990. The basic reason for this Report, is an attempt to reduce the unacceptable levels of economic inequalities, poverty commonly experienced in the less developing countries and even certain neglected regions of a large and developed country. Adequate attention need to be paid to these aspects related to development experience in the less developing nations, because as Myrdal (1984) highlights that "what is needed to raise the miserable living levels of the poor masses is instead radical institutional reforms. These would serve the double purpose of greater equality and economic growth". Tinbergen also emphasizes the importance of substantial income transfer to correct the present income differences between the rich and the poor. Study of human development therefore emphasises the need to achieve social justice and enhance human happiness for which we need to create institutions that transmute the longing for a better world into a set of policies, which begin by raising the welfare of the deprived sections.

Economic growth and well-being of the common man as measured by Human Development are, therefore, not contradictory, as some economists wrongly tend to opine. In fact, they are complimentary and no economic growth can be initiated and sustained at low level of human development just as high-level of human development can only be sustained, with resources obtained through high rate of economic growth. Growth does not automatically transform itself into human development. All depends on the nature and extent to which policies and programmes of an economy are geared to harmonize economic growth with human development. Achieving these two goals simultaneously should form part of every development goal and effort. It is here that the role of the state assumes importance and the study of human development assumes significance from the point of view of policy perspective. The widespread criticism of Trickle Down Theory which has proved ineffective for most parts of the country in the Indian context, can be made a meaningful exercise through changing the entire perspective of policy formulation. As Haq (1996) opines that under the circumstances the focus of attention of most policies would be the people rather than production only. Policies according to him should contain certain elements missing from most of the policies today. For instance, policies should begin with a detailed profile of its people in terms of education, health, poverty, cultural and political aspirations and all other factors that go to constitute a good quality of life. This exercise should be undertaken both for rural and urban divide, and also for various social, religious and most importantly across spatial dimension. Lack of knowledge about the people, for whom policies are to be formulated, cannot be expected to provide satisfactory results. Hence, our present study assumes crucial significance from this point of view.

Haq further opines that policy makers must first decide upon the ends and device the means accordingly. They should decide the basic human needs of the society in terms of nutrition, health, education housing, transport etc. and only then the targets of physical production can be made. This necessitates integration of production policies of equitable distribution. Equal emphasis even if not greater emphasis should be put on policies which ensures equitable distribution of the national product. Policies focusing human development should also make people equal partners in development. Encouragement should, therefore, be provided to people to participate in development process. Assessment of the progress of an economy should be made from the point of view of not only the macro economic indicators, but also the social indicators which are the basic tenets of Human Development paradigm. It is only then that development efforts can be made more meaningful. In fact, such growth models can ensure sustainable development. The basic forces of market economy, ensuring optimum allocation of resources can no doubt be satisfied, but the human crisis of the pure neo-classical model of growth cannot be overlooked either. The problem of development in modern world is not only multi-dimensional but unique as well.

At the same time, it is also crucial to focus attention to the fact that too much emphasis on either economic growth or only human development may result in unbalanced growth of the economy, which may once again jeopardize the very process of long term sustainable development (Sengupta, 2002). Sustaining the process of development is the pivotal issue of Human Development paradigm. If any state or region have to survive on aid from the centre on a permanent basis, sustainability of developmental efforts in the region will be seriously impaired. Making the growth process sustainable by emphasizing on human development implies that enough of the resources created at present should be invested in education and health of today's generation. These people in turn may sustain the process of economic development of the future generations also, so that the future generation need not pay the debts of today's generation. Therefore, sustaining human life is more important. Sustenance of the physical environment such as the ecological environment or the economy are only means to sustain human life.

The main tenets of the paradigm of human development are, therefore, the people. Every aspect of economic development is assessed from the point of view of the people. The objective of growth is the betterment of people's lives and not merely expansion of production processes. This paradigm further necessitates that people should not only build capabilities, by building their health, education and skills, but must also be provided with all the opportunities to use up these capabilities through adequate employment opportunities. Full expansion of the GDP and the macro-economic variables which are considered as means of economic development are as important as the end, which are the people. Apart from the pure economic factors, non-economic factors such as the political, cultural and social factors also play an equally important role in determining human development.

In the 1950s and 1960s many nations had experienced economic development, yet the living conditions of the masses remained extremely deplorable. It was only in the seventies that realisation dawned upon the planners and policy makers that benefits of development did not trickle down to the masses. The fact that development was purely an economic phenomenon in which the GNP growth would trickle down to the masses, for the wider distribution of economic and social benefits of growth, did not seem to work. This resulted in discarding GNP as a true indicator of growth. Direct attack on poverty, low level of living, inequitable income distribution and rising unemployment, were the pivotal issues which were incorporated in the new concept of Human Development, and were gradually forming part of development plans and policies. Similar was the view of the World Bank, which during the eighties championed economic growth as the goal of development and had taken a much broader view of development. This is evident from 1991 World Development Report, in which it maintained that "the challenge of development is to improve the quality of life. Especially in the world's poor countries, a better quality of life generally calls for higher incomes—but it involves much more. It encompasses as ends in themselves better education, higher standards of health and nutrition, less poverty, a cleaner environment more equality of opportunity, greater individual freedom and a richer cultural life."

Multi-dimensional aspect of the process of development is, therefore, accepted by most planners and policy-makers. This modern dimension of development, involves major changes in social structure, attitudes, national institutions, eradication of poverty, raising the levels of living, along with acceleration of economic growth. "Development, in its essence, must represent the whole gamut of change by which an entire social system turned to the diverse basic needs and desires of individuals and social groups, within that system, moves away from a condition of life widely perceived as unsatisfactory towards a situation or condition of life regarded as materially and spiritually better" (Todaro and Smith, 2003).

The fact that it has still not been possible to solve the problems of hunger, illiteracy, malnutrition and poverty in major parts of the country, where the condition of quality of life in most places is much lower than the all India level, only reveals the choice of wrong strategy of development. The assumption of the Trickle Down Theory has totally failed in the region like the rest of India. Western paradigms are, therefore, no longer accepted blindly with the same degree of fervour. Voices of disagreement have characterized the nations of the Third World countries, who in turn slowly and gradually started adopting their own development paradigm. Development experience of China, can be cited as a wonderful example. The developmentalists of the western paradigm are now considered "as false prophets whose faulty paradigm led to massive misdirection of effort" (Dube, 1988).

The result of all the futile efforts over the years, at developing the economy, particularly that of the North East reveal that we have once again to rediscover the basic truth of all development strategy—that people should occupy the centre-stage of all development. Even in India itself, different states have developed at different rates, in spite of similar physical investment. States with rich natural resources or heavy capital investment, have not displayed any satisfactory record in terms of economic development. In contrast, some states with insufficient resources, both natural as well as financial, have performed much better, because the people of those states have greater capability and are therefore much more hard working and efficient. The name of Kerala emerges as the most important example. The north eastern region in India, is one of the richest in the endowment of unique type of natural resources, yet the extent of economic development is one of the lowest in the whole country. The crucial factor that can be identified here are the people, and their skills, ability and capability which make the major difference to development. Therefore, it will be futile to think of developing a nation/region without developing the people themselves. This has been the fallacy of development of the entire country, over the past decades. Though the rest of the country has realized this error and talking more in terms of placing the people at the centre stage of development, similar realization has yet to dawn on the planners and policy makers of some other parts of the country. People are yet to be placed at the centre stage of development. The task is indeed a formidable one, since the region is characterized by diverse ethnic, religious and linguistic groups, and the record of economic development so far has also not been very encouraging either.

New Development Paradigm

Mahbul-ul-Haq who is considered the father of the concept of human development opines that the new paradigm of development should be the **Human Development paradigm**. The basic objective of development is to create an environment for people to enable them to enjoy a long and healthy life. Increase in GNP saving, investment, trade, business and other macro economic indicators of growths are important to the extent that they contribute and act as means of raising the quality of life of the people. Once these people acquire the required capability they can contribute further for raising the macro economic indicators of the country/region. It is, therefore, crucial for policy makers to understand the circular relationship between human development and economic development. This strategy of development is extremely important from the point of view of this region, as people seem to be alienating themselves more and more from the process of development.

Haq also opines that basic purpose of all development is to enlarge people's choices, which relates to accessibility to knowledge, nutrition and health services, security of life and property, political, cultural and religions freedom. All these may not be revealed statistics of a region, but are extremely vital for the people, who will in the long-run ultimately contribute to increase the growth statistics of the region (Mahbul-ul-Haq, 1996). Therefore, every aspect of economic development contributes in enlarging human development.

The publication of the Human Development Report by UNDP and the pioneering work of Sen, Mahbul-ul-Haq and others have brought about a change in the development paradigm. The new development economics, contribute a positive paradigm shift from neo-classical economics. It challenges the latter's faith in Pareto optimality and competitive market which are unable to explain the distributional aspect of economic growth. Developing economics including that of India, can find solutions to the problems of abject poverty, if they base their policies on development economics. This is because the core idea of development economics is reconciliation of economic growth with improving the distribution of income and eradication of the worst form of poverty. Reduction of inequality and poverty necessitates a sustained rate of growth of per capita income, which can in turn enable channelization of resources from the rich to the poor. At the same time, reduction of poverty and inequality can also expedite the growth process. Income distribution following a regressive pattern under extreme poverty and inequality depresses consumption demand, making the accelerator-multiplier work in the reverse direction, which in turn depresses the growth rate.

Development economics can therefore be clearly distinguished from distributionally insensitive neo-classical economics. Its direct concern with policy related issues also makes it distinct from neo-classical school, the main focus of which has very little connection with real life problems of economics. Growth with sustainable human development is thus the shift in paradigm, rather than only growth. The present paradigm of growth is therefore much broader. It emphasizes the basic issue that efforts of development administration to alleviate poverty through economic growth and redistribution of income and wealth would be meaningless without an expansion of basic capabilities of the people of the region or the country.

As has already been highlighted earlier, the Trickle Down Theory proved totally ineffective in tackling problems of mass poverty, illiteracy, ill-health and malnutrition. It was clearly evident that something must have gone wrong somewhere. It was clear that if development strategy from top to bottom did not work, surely the strategy of emphasizing the reverse direction needs to be given greater attention. This will help in identification of the inadequacies of the basic living conditions of the common man. The horizon of economic development as a result of this changed perception, consisted of the development of social infrastructure like education, health, nutrition, access to sanitation and drinking water. Economic growth is essential only to the extent that it is able to sustain these social objectives in the long run. Policy makers and planners now assess the success of their plans from the point of view of not only economic growth, but also from the point of view of achievement of these social indicators.

Though eradication of poverty and attainment of economic equality and social justice have been the objectives of the successive. Five Year Plans in India, yet it was only the Eighth Plan which identified human development as its primary objective. The plan emphasized the creation of jobs, eradication of illiteracy, universalisation of elementary education, provision of safe drinking water and primary health care facilities to all. The Ninth Five Year Plan too reiterated its emphasis on human development and focused the importance of all public action towards that objective. Keeping the objectives of the Five Year Plans in view and also governed by the publication of the successive Reports on Human Development, various state governments have undertaken the publication of Human Development Reports of the respective states. The NCAER too published Human Development Report of India for the nineties. The Planning Commission also prepared its National Human Development Report in 2001. The realization has, therefore, dawned upon the planners and policy-makers that human development should be the prime focus of all development policies.

The new development paradigm therefore attempts to capture all these vital issues relating to human development, and is popularly known as new development economics. It is not a deviation from main stream economics, but it surely deals with the multi-dimensional complexity of the process of economic development, and not just economic growth. It deals mainly with the accumulation of physical and human capital, progress of skills, merging of ideas, growth of population, the manner in which the produced and non produced factors of production are combined and managed to initiate and sustain growth, offering sensible remedies to resolve this complexity to every one's advantage (Naqvi, 2002). This branch of study is concerned mainly with the process that tend to raise per capita income over time and distribute it more equitably by an overall transformation of the structure of demand, trade, production and employment (Chenery, 1981).

The new paradigm further focuses on the "ought questions" rather than the "is questions". The latter issue excludes all matters which does not deal with self-interest maximization since it is irrational, because it is ethical. However, ethical considerations highlight the crucial development and global concerns such as poverty, distributional inequities and unemployment which is absent in the "is question" of positive economics. The "ought question" of the new development paradigm leading to a more just social order in which the needs of the least privileged sections are looked after in the best possible manner, need not be mixed up with Marxist economics. Economic growth is an instrument of equitable distribution of the fruits of progress so that people have an opportunity to lead a minimum acceptable life.

Study of human development in the context of this new development economics, is therefore rapidly evolving in its own right as a distinctive analytical tool of study. The economics of contemporary poor nations with varying ideological orientations, cultural backgrounds are very complex, yet similar economic problems demand new ideas. Development economics, using the tool of human development is more concerned with the economic, cultural and political requirements, so that the fruits of economic development can be distributed to the major segment of the society. Role of government assumes importance and to some extent coordinated economic decision-making for transforming the economy is an essential component of this new paradigm.

Though developed economies do not deal with perfect markets of advanced capitalist economies, where least cost allocation of scarce productive resources and with the optimal growth of these resources to produce an ever expanding range of goods and services, assumes the main focuses of our study. Marginal analysis and private profit maximization and utility analysis are the main tools of analysis of the traditional school. New development economics in contrast, combines relevant concepts and theories from traditional economic analysis along with new models and broader multi-disciplinary approaches derived from studying the historical and contemporary development experience of developing countries. Development economics therefore assumes greater role in economically backward nations/regions. Problems are analyzed within the context of the overall social system of a country. Social system implies interdependent relationships between economic and non-economic factors. Non-economic factors include attitudes towards life, work, legal and administrative structure, pattern of kinship and religion, cultural traditions, systems of land tenures, participation in development decision and activities, and the flexibility and rigidity of economic classes. The factors vary widely from one society to another and from one culture to another. Raising economic indicators of growth are all functions of local history, expectations, values incentives, attitudes and belief. North East region is characterized by wide diversity with respect to socio-cultural traits, with many ethnic groups, tribes and sub-tribes, with ways and attitude towards life, production, cultivation, which are in total dichotomy with mainstream life. Though a section of the social scientists dismiss these non-economic variables as "non-quantifiable" and therefore, unimportant from the point of view of study of economics, but the new development economics assigns an important role to the non-economic factors in determining and shaping the course of economic events. In fact, most of the development problems of low level of human development, inequality and poverty in different parts of the world, have arisen mainly due to the negligence of these important issues for years.

It is due to these reasons that the general economic models have very little relevance to the real life problems of developing countries. Since economics studies human relationship in the social context, economic models are subject to great variations in different societies, cultures and at different times. Value concepts, unlike the views of the traditional school, becomes the pivotal focus of new development economics. Incorporation of social equality, eradication of poverty raising the levels of living are issues which relate to value judgement and thereby tackling these issues differ from place to place and from one culture and society to another. Study of economics, therefore, cannot be totally value neutral, as assumed by the traditional school of economics. Once the policy-makers come to a consensus relating to these socio-economic goals, the corresponding public policies like taxing the higher income group of people, based on "objective" theoretical and quantitative analysis can be adopted (Todaro, 2003).

It is, therefore, evident that economic problems of less developed regions/nations cannot be viewed from the same perspective of pure economic models applicable easily to developed ones. In less developing regions, interdependent relationship between economic and non-economic factors assume great significance. Non-economic factors include, many important issues, like degree of popular participation in development decisions assumes flexibility as well as rigidity of the social classes. All these factors vary from one region to another, from one culture to another and from one social setting to another, increasing the significance of new development economics as against the traditional economics.

It was due to all these reasons that from 1970s onwards economic development was viewed from a new perspective. The focus was in elimination of poverty, inequality and unemployment. Redistribution from growth became a common slogan. Dudley Seers therefore while examining the issue of development maintains that "The question to ask about a country's development are therefore: what has been happening to poverty ? What has been happening to inequality ? If all of these have declined from high levels, then beyond doubt this has been a period of development for the country concerned. If one or two of these central problems have been growing worse, especially if all have, it would be strange to call the result "development", even if per capita income is doubled.

This approach to economics was necessitated by the rising per capita income on one hand, but worsening level of poverty and unemployment on the other, witnessed during the sixties and seventies of the last century. The early seventies therefore witnessed the need for a change in approach of pure economics. Development experience particularly of those of the less developed nations have revealed that economic development has to have a multi-dimensional approach, the essence of which must represent the whole gamut of change, by which an entire social system, attuned to the diverse basic needs and desires of individuals and social groups within that system needs to move away from a condition of life, characterized by misery to better condition of life.

No work on the new development paradigm can be complete without mentioning the views of the leading thinker on this line, namely Amartya Sen. Sen postulates that "Economic growth cannot be sensibly treated as an end in itself. Development has to be more concerned with enhancing the quality of life we lead and the freedoms we enjoy". Utility approach of traditional economics does not make much of a sense, for human well-being according to Sen. It is the functioning that is what a person does with the commodities of given characteristics that they come to possess or control. Freedom of choice, so that one can have control over ones own life is the essence of Sen's approach to human well-being. Income or consumption are highly subjective and therefore cannot define well-being in any adequate sense. Real appraisal of well-being leads to a consideration of health and education as well as income.

All these arguments reinforced by Sen's approach to human welfare, has resulted in the publication of the annual Human Development Report, using the important tool of human development index, with education, health and income as the indicators to measure the well-being of the people of a nation.

UNDP's Human Development Index

The United Nations Development Programme (UNDP) in its annual series of Human Development Report has made a pioneering and ambitious effort to incorporate the various indicators of a good quality of life, into a single index, known as the Human Development Index (HDI) since 1990. The index analyses the comparative status of socio-economic development in both developed and developing nations systematically and comprehensively. Since 1990, every year refinement of the index is undertaken. The construction of the index, accepts three indicators like health cducation, and per capita income which it considers as the three goals or end products of development. Indicator of health is measured by life-expectancy at birth, education or knowledge is measured by a weighted average of adult literacy (two-third) and standard of living as measured by real per capita income.

An important contribution of HDI is that it focuses attention to the fact that a nation may have a high level of income, but may fare badly in terms of human development. In contrast, a nation may perform poorly in terms of economic development but may do much better in human development. A clear example is that of the state of Kerala whose economic performance is rather insignificant against its impressive performance in terms of human development. One of the most significant contribution of HDI is that it highlights the important fact that development does not mean only rise in income but it implies broad human development. It reveals that though there is a tendency for the convergence in health and education for most nations, yet great disparity in income is a characteristic feature of most others. Another important contribution of HDR report is that detailed analysis of health and education reveals that they are not merely components of human capital and production inputs as has been maintained earlier. These factors are fundamental development goals in their own right.

The Human Development Index has successfully revealed through its detailed study that a nation of high income individuals who are not literate and have low health status may have lower life expectancy and thereby lead a short life. In contrast, a nation with low income individuals may achieve a higher level of development which has individuals who are literate and have good health status. A better indicator of development disparity and rankings might be found by including health and education variables in a weighted welfare measure rather than by looking only at income levels. The use of HDI can also show at a disaggregative level the HDI between men and women, different social classes reflecting different income distribution and different regions and ethnic groups.

In keeping with the basic ideas of new development economics the UNDP's Human Development Report has made valuable contributions in focusing to the core idea of development, and the nations which are improving in this respect. It also highlights how different socio-economic groups and regions within countries perform in this respect. As per the basic principles of new development economics, by combining social and economic data, HDI allows nations to take a broader measure of their development performance. Such issues may, therefore, enable reorientation of their economic and social policies more directly on those areas which require special developmental efforts. A proper synchronisation of HDI with traditional economic measures of development, enables us to understand, which countries are achieving development in the real sense of the term. By analysing the various components of HDI in general and for different sub-groups of the society we are able to understand to what extent a country is developing and to what extent each group is benefiting as well as participating in that process of development.

Human Development and Economic Development

However, a word of caution also needs to be mentioned here. Development strategy may be growth led, by creating an initial favourable condition for people's participation as was the case in China. It may be growth led with unfavourable initial condition, and corrective public policies at a later stage as has happened in Malayasia. The other strategy may be strong emphasis on public policy to provide social services but with low growth. Such a strategy, however, is unsustainable over the long period. This strategy was adopted in Jamaica, Sri Lanka and Kerala in India. The Kerala model, with high level of human development but a stagnant economy has become a matter of great controversy in development context. In developed economies where growth models are launched with an already satisfactory achievement in social indicator, further spending on these items, enables the economy to reach the take-off stage. Consequently, when people reach a high level of human development, they are able to look after and spend for their own socio-economic needs. This enables the government to concentrate on economic growth, leaving the people to spend for themselves. Consequently, expenditure on social sector declines after a certain point. However, in a less developed economy with a low level of per capita income, people tend to have a dependency syndrome, and they expect the government to continuously spend for them. This is one of the factors responsible for the paradox of the Kerala model.

A school of thought has therefore developed which erroneously opines that spending scarce resources for raising human development would only be at the cost of economic development, particularly for a less developed nation. However, it needs to be realised by economists as well as social workers that economic development and human development are not contradictory, in fact they are both complimentary. It is, therefore, extremely essential to understand the meaning of this concept. Human Development does not confine itself merely in pushing up the statistical figures on health, education and other socio-economic indicators. Such a narrow view of human development would make all efforts at raising human development totally meaningless, with an extremely short-run connotation. The concept of human development is much wider. Human Development is a process of enlarging people's choices (HDR, 1995). Enlarging people's choices is, therefore, not confined to any specific period, but spills over several generations. The main purpose of human development is to prepare the people, to have access to resources needed to lead a decent standard of living. This preparation takes the form of acquiring knowledge and good health. They should also have political, economic, social and cultural freedom. The HRD of 1995, therefore, maintains that Human Development has two sides. Hence much of the misunderstanding between economic and human development has arisen in the past. The concept of Human Development is much broader than the traditional theories of economic development. Even the welfare theories of economic development fail to capture the essence of Human Development. Welfare approaches of economic theories consider people as the beneficiaries of economic development. It attempts to provide material goods and services to deprived population, rather than in enlarging human choices in all fields.

The concept of human development is much broader since it brings together production and distribution of commodities along with the expansion and use of human capabilities. Therefore, all aspects, of the economy, including economic growth, trade, employment, political freedom or cultural values are viewed from the perspective of the people. Economic growth and human development are therefore not contradictory and cannot be viewed in isolation. The achievement of one is impossible without the achievement of the other. Attainment of Human Development is impossible without economic growth, since resources required for raising Human Development can be acquired only through a high rate of economic growth. An impoverished nation, with insufficient resources, has to make extra efforts to acquire resources for raising Human Development. This, however, is not to suggest, that economic development and human development are highly correlated.

It also needs to be highlighted that economic growth by itself is meaningless without Human Development. If the fruits of development are concentrated only in a few hands, economic development would be meaningless. Experience has revealed that nations who do not concentrate on Human Development have witnessed growing concentration of income in a few hands. Economic growth by itself cannot automatically transform itself into higher levels of Human Development. All depend on how the policies can be geared to achieve such objectives.

Human Development and Economic Development are thus not contradictory, rather they are more of a complimentary nature. It is therefore essential to overcome the misconception harboured by critics of Human Development, that stress on it, is at the cost of economic growth. At the same time, it is also crucial to focus attention to the fact that too much emphasis on either economic growth or Human Development alone might result in unbalanced growth of the economy, which may jeopardize the very process of long-term economic development.

REFERENCES

Chenery (1983): "Interaction between theory and observation in Development", *World Development*.

Dube (1988): "*Modernization and Development*": *The Search for Alternative Paradigms*, Vistar Publication, New Delhi.

Haq, Mahbul-ul (1996): "*Reflections on Human Development*", OUP.

Kunda, A. Pradhan and Subramanian (2002): "Dichotomy or Continuum: Analysis of Impact of Urban Centres on their Periphery", *Economic and Political Weekly*, Vol. 37.

Myrdal, G., (1984): "*Pioneer in Development*", OUP, New York.

Naqvi, S.N.H. (2002): *Development Economics—Nature and Significance*, Sage Publications, New Delhi.

NCAER: *Human Development Report*.

Planning Commission (2001): *National Human Development Report*.

Putman, R. (1993): "*Making Democracy Work: Civic Traders in Modern Italy*." Princeton University Press, Princeton, New York.

Sengupta, K. (2002): "Indian Economy: Economic Growth and Human Development". *Man and Development.* Vol., Chandigarh.

Todaro and Smith, F. (2003): "*Economic Development*", Pearson Education, Delhi, India.

UNDP (1990; 1995): *Human Development Reports*. OUP, New York.

World Bank (1991): "World Development Report (WDR) 1991", (The Challenge of Development), New York, OUP.

Section Two

Human Development and Economic Development

2

Human Development and the Indian Context

PULIN B. NAYAK

Introduction

The Indian economy is currently on a high growth trajectory. The recent 9 per cent plus growth rate of GDP that we have been able to achieve is largely a result of the economic liberalization and the reform measures which were initiated about a decade and a half back. There are several other positive features of the recent growth process which ought to be noted. The tax to GDP ratio, after a dip in the early years of reform, is now again back to around 16.5 per cent of GDP, and appears to be on an upward trend. The gross domestic savings rate is now around 32.4 per cent of GDP, an increase of as many as 9 percentage points of GDP during the last 5 years. Assuming an economy-wide capital output ratio in the range of about 4 and using the simple Harrod-Domar formulation, we appear to be set for a growth rate figure in the range of around 8 per cent plus. All of these are positive tidings.

However, despite nearly six decades of planned economic development and the recent record of high growth rates, the fact remains that the human development indicators in India continue to be abysmally low. India is home to the largest numbers of the poor and the destitute. The indicators in terms of infant mortality and women's education and nutritional levels are among the poorest in the world. India also has among the lowest female to male sex ratios in the world today. The recent growth experience has paradoxically not resulted in high growth rates of jobs, giving rise to the phenomenon of 'jobless growth'. There is considerable regional variation in the development indicators, and some parts of the country have been virtually bypassed from the developmental process. A vast majority of the poor are concentrated amongst the socially backward sections of society. It would be desirable to look at the developmental process from both an economic as well as a sociological perspective. It is imperative that we reappraise the entire developmental process afresh.

Some Selected Features of the Indian Economy

At the very beginning it might not be out of place to briefly take a look at the broad sectoral growth figures. The 2006-07 growth rate of 9.2 per cent has been principally driven by the growth rate of 11.2 per cent in the services sector and 10.0 per cent in the industrial sector. Agriculture, in contrast, has grown only at about 2.7 per cent. Around the time of Independence agriculture accounted for about 60 per cent of GDP, but its share has now come down to as low as 19 per cent. Services and industry now respectively account for about 54 and 27 per cent of GDP respectively. The problem however is that agriculture continues to be the mainstay of nearly 60 per cent of the country's population. This clearly implies that the sectoral per capita incomes have been widening quite sharply, with the agriculturists faring poorly *vis-à-vis* those in the services and the industry sectors.

Reports of suicide deaths by farmers are no longer isolated instances. In addition to the early reports coming in from the dry land tracts of Andhra Pradesh and Maharashtra, one now comes across reports of such deaths from Rajasthan, Punjab, Madhya Pradesh and yet some other parts of the country. In parts of Punjab and Maharashtra the exposure of agriculture to the lure of cash crops has exposed it to greater degrees of risk due to disease and pestilence and some of the instances of suicides are clearly due to this factor. Most of the deaths occur in situations where a farmer would have taken a relatively small loan which he is unable to repay and cannot bear the sense of ignominy. This contrast starkly with the situation in some large industrial houses where there are instances of loans of hundreds of crores that have not been repaid but with the loanees continuing to lead perfectly regular and even luxurious lives. In addition to the purely economic factors there are deeper sociological reasons involving familial honour and morality that leads the hapless farmers to take this drastic step.

In contrast, the industrial and services sectors seem to be on a secular upswing. Corporate salaries are scaling dizzying heights and the stock market has gone past the 17000 mark. The success of the upper end of the services sector comprising the Information Technology (IT) sector and banking etc., however must not mask the reality that the employment potential of this sector is minimal, being confined to the graduates of engineering and management schools. They make only a marginal difference to the stock of the unemployed in the economy at large. As per the Economic Survey 2006-07 the annual growth of employment in the organized sector during 1994-2004 was in the negative range, the figure being (minus) 0.38. Graduates of well established business schools can command hefty starting packages, and are the toast of the upper middle class population as well as the market survey media. The contrast with the mass of unemployed youth in small towns and villages dotted all over the country is too stark and has all the elements of societal malaise if not explosion.

The key to any meaningful remedy must involve a massive investment in the agriculture sector to substantially raise farm productivity. The other strategy must be to bolster the share of manufacturing, now comprising about 16 per cent of GDP. It is manufacturing which is the dynamic component of the industrial sector. In China industry comprises 47 per cent of its GDP, of which manufacturing accounts for about 33 per cent. The Chinese growth rate of about 9.5 to 10 per cent, sustained over a quarter century is substantially driven by its manufacturing sector, which has the capacity to absorb substantial volumes of labour, both skilled as well as unskilled. This is a matter of no small importance in low wage economies like ours. Our services led growth has the important disadvantage of not being able to generate employment in the formal sector especially in the low skill categories. Most of the growth of employment in recent years has been in the casual and non-formal sectors. For the vast bulk of the population, with little or virtually nil wealth, other than their labour power, unemployment automatically implies poverty and even destitution. And it is in such circumstances that education and health take a back seat and human development indicators reach their nadir.

Human Development Indicators for India

At US $720, for the year 2005, India has one of the lowest per capita income levels in the world (*cf.* World Development Report, 2007). The comparable figure for China was US$1740. India and China both had about the same level of per capita income in 1982. It is a measure of the extraordinary success of the Chinese developmental process that they are as far ahead as they are today, not only in terms of per capita income but also in terms of some of the most basic human development indicators in the areas of health, education, women and children's nutrition, among others.

Despite our sustained effort at conscious development planning going back to the early 1950s, inspired by the thoughts and writings of Pandit Jawaharlal Nehru and other notablc planners including Prasanta Mahalanobis and Pitambar Pant, India's showing in terms of the widely used Human Development Index (HDI) as developed by the UNDP continues to be far from satisfactory, to say the least. Some of the factors that are crucial in the computation of the HDI are life expectancy at birth, adult literacy rate, GDP per capita and enrolment ratio for primary, secondary and tertiary schools, (see the Human Development Report 2006, UNDP). In the year 2006 India's rank was as low as 126 in a listing of some 177 countries. Among the countries that preceded us in the ranking were Nicaragua, Bolivia, Honduras and Namibia, to name just a few, and also to be conscious of our humble position in the comity of nations from this very important standpoint. This also flies in the face of those amongst us who choose to be complacent in their assessment that after a decade and a half of economic reforms India has now arrived and is one of the major 'players' in the world.

India's performance is particularly poor when it comes to any of the gender related indicators such as gender inequality in education, gender inequality in economic activity or any broad and familiar measure of women's empowerment. We have among the worst indicators in respect of under-five mortality rate, maternal mortality rate and births attended by skilled health staff as a percentage of total births. India's sex ratio is lower than many of the sub-Saharan African countries that are poorer to us in terms of per capita income. And the irony is that the ratio is getting worse and has even dipped the 900 mark in some of our dynamic states like Punjab and Haryana that are the higher ones in terms of per capita state domestic product (SDP).

A matter of no small importance is the need for equity in the regional development of a country. If over a substantial length of time developmental efforts and resources are confined to special privileged pockets the system soon becomes unviable. The lack of adequate development in the North East is one of the glaring failures of a system of planning that has privileged the metropolises like Delhi and Mumbai to the exclusion of remote areas that have lacked the political clout. The destabilising consequences of this process are obvious for all of us to see. With globalisation and instant communication the aspiration levels of especially the youth are rapidly increasing. Unless there are adequate channels of directing these youth to avenues of meaningful work and vocation the social consequences may be substantially more destabilising than they have been ever before.

Understanding the Process of Human Development

The root cause of the low levels of human development is the prevalence of widespread and abysmal poverty. It is also certainly the case that the causation goes in the reverse direction too. The provisional data of the NSS 61st round for the year 2004-05 indicates that the poverty ratio was 27.8 per cent if the Uniform Recall Period is used. It is also well known that while the above percentage denotes the population that is absolutely poor, there is another band, at least another quarter of the population that is on the margins of survival. This is corroborated by some recent empirical exercises which seem to suggest that if one were to think of an expenditure of Rs. 20 per day as the absolute minimum required by an adult, then as much as 77 per cent of the population of the country would have to be regarded as poor. Admittedly 23 per cent of a large population base as in our case would mean sizable absolute numbers who might give the necessary dynamism to the domestic consumer good sector. Yet the fact remains that, if true, this would be a strong indictment of the entire paradigm of development that we have adopted up till now.

It also so happens that of the poor population so identified the overwhelming majority, almost four-fifths, belong to the socially backward classes, comprising the bottom rungs in the caste hierarchy as well as religious minorities. If we have to think in terms of eradicating poverty it would be futile to regard it as a purely economic problem. That the sociological aspects of the developmental process are also integrally important has been emphasised by scholars from Marx to Schumpeter. Schumpeter had argued for looking at the 'socio-economic' aspects of the development process in addition to confining it to the purely political economy.

If such be the rather poor state of affairs the question arises whether we are left with nothing but despair on the development front and whether something may yet not be done when the polity has just celebrated sixty years of its independence. Quite clearly we need to have a reappraisal of the entire process of development afresh. In order to be meaningful clearly the process of development has to be inclusive, and one needs to have development with dignity.

At the very base of everything else is the right to basic livelihood. Towards this possibly the most innovative programme initiated by the government has got to be the National Rural Employment Guarantee Scheme (NREGS) which allows for 100 days of paid labour in the vicinity of a person's place of residence. The scheme was operationalised in early 2005. The key idea of the scheme is to give cash wage in return for a full day's work to anyone willing to offer himself or herself to manual labour. There has been substantial opposition to the scheme from certain well heeled economists and other academic experts of the country on the ground that the scheme would be fiscally wasteful, and that it would lead to corruption. If corruption were truly to be the key deciding factor then surely the entire governmental machinery would have to be closed down forthwith. As regards the fiscal waste, one should ponder the fact that the non-performing assets (NPAs) of the banking sector in the country at large amount to as much as Rs. 80,000 crores and the list of the defaulters reads like a who's who of the top industrial houses of the country.

There are already some early evaluations of the scheme and what we have is a mixed picture. The scheme is to be operationalised with the active participation of the panchayats and the Gram Sabhas along with the governmental district and block level functionaries. Where the organisers of the scheme are individuals with a certain social purpose and commitment the scheme seems to be already showing positive results. But there are also enough reports of utter failure and siphoning off of funds. These are invariably in those parts where there is the usual cynical and vile bureaucracy, entrenched local interest groups and an absence of political will.

A very recent report in *The Hindu* is highly revealing. A certain Rupa Majhi, a poor advasi of Palsipada village in Kalahandi district in Orissa was given 21 days of employment and paid Rs. 600 as wages during 2006-07. This would be an average of under Rs. 30 per day, an amount well below the minimum wage. The work was on a road construction project under the NREGS. On his job card however it is falsely written that he had worked for 336 days. The online job card of Rupa Majhi posted on the NREGS website has a third version of work and payment details. And it is this: that Rupa Majhi was given 102 days of wage employment and paid Rs. 6,310 as wages. This means that out of Rs. 6310, only Rs. 600 actually came in the hands of Rupa Majhi. The remaining Rs. 5710, which is more than 90 per cent of the total wage payment made in the name of Rupa Majhi, has been siphoned off and misappropriated by the government officials. There are similar stories from some other parts of the country as well.

Concluding Remarks

Under the Right to Information (RTI) Act the worker has the right to inspect his or her muster roll. If the person is illiterate and himself or herself not in a position to do so, one can expect some panchayat level workers or NGO volunteers to help. There is nothing in the governmental machinery that says that there cannot be a social audit which goes into the full details of a case such as this, fixes responsibility and takes firm and drastic action against errant officials. But all of this calls for a heightened sense of social and political awareness and a keenness to work with a social purpose. This can only be brought about when the dispossessed begin to think of shaping their own destiny with the resources and the strengths that they have at their own disposal. In short, they need to be vested with a sense of empowerment. This can only happen when they are well fed, well clothed, are healthy and educated so that they can lead meaningful lives. Just as the rights to life and liberty are regarded as basic we must also think of the right to development as a basic and fundamental right. The constituents of this right would include some minimum levels of income, education and health to all the citizens. It is incumbent on every modern state to ensure this right to its citizens.

3

Towards a Human Development Strategy: Case for Re-prioritization of Public Expenditure in India

SIBRANJAN MISRA

> "*Since premature mortality, significant undernourishment and widespread illiteracy are deprivations that directly impoverish human life, the allocation of economic resources as well as arrangements for social provision must give some priority to removing these disadvantages for the affected population.*"
>
> —Amartya Sen, "Economic Policy and Enquiry: An Overview in Economic Policy and Equity," ed. by Vito Tanzi, Ke-young Chu and Sanjeev Gupta (Washington: International Monetary Fund), 1999

Human resources are the real wealth of the nation. In any country, there can be no meaningful economic development without aggregate human capital. The human dimension is the sine qua non of economic recovery. This idea has led a group of economists to define Human Development as a process of enlarging people's choices and opportunities as well as raising the levels of well being. In fact, these choices may be infinite. The choice to live a long and healthy life, the choice to acquire knowledge and to have access to resources necessary for a decent living are recognised as the most socially valuable factors. The importance of higher real income in generating possibilities of living worthwhile lives which are not possible at lower levels of income cannot be denied. These are estimates which often suggest that nearly half of the variations in the life expectancy could be attributed to differences in GNP per head. The effect of higher per capita GNP on, for example, life expectancy or better literacy level or low mortality rates among children works via effects in which public policy stance plays a significant role.

However, there is a need for designing some strong and credible policy initiatives towards evolving an inclusive and stable political economy which will ensure quality growth, job opportunities and balanced human development.

1. There exists a wide range of ways and means of achieving success in human development and hence, there is no unique path. What really promotes human development? Growth of per capita income is generally recognised as a measure of improving human development. But there are also some other empirical studies which reveal that per capita income cannot be a sole determinant of achieving human development. It is argued that public spending also has a significant role to play. However, one strand of liberal paradigm has been encouraging economic growth as a prerequisite for investment in human development. Human development may be postponed until economic resource expansion makes it affordable (Williamson, 1993; Ravallion, 1997). The other strand strongly viewed a consistent strategy promoting both objectives simultaneously and supporting key issues like social expenditure, female literacy, equity in income distribution, etc. (White, 1999; Ranis *et al*, 2000; Ranis and Stuart, 2005). This strand identifies a fundamental two-way links between the economic growth and human development. Human development can be promoted directly or indirectly via policies and programmes which promote income growth.

It is true that advances in growth theory and human capital literature and thereby basic needs as well as capabilities approaches have shown the complexities and varieties of synergies in which economic prosperity and level of human development can affect each other (Ranis and Stewart, 2000).

In most of the developing countries, there exist two chains—one, from economic growth to human development and the other, from human development to economic growth. Those countries are trapped within the vicious circle—below average human development and economic growth. Growth and human development are not coherent, rather lopsided. The countries with lopsided development expenditure tend to fall over time into a vicious cycle. Neither lopsided situation is sustainable over periods. Both types refer to unstable equilibrium.

The link and causality between human development and economic growth has been of crucial importance. Empirical evidences on the causality are abundant. Under the purview of endogenous growth models, the close association between human development and economic growth is clearly recognised. There are different studies which documented the high association between economic growth and human/social indicators. The higher the level of education of workforce, the higher the overall productivity of capital; because, the more educated are likely to innovate which improves overall productivity (Lucas, 1990; Romar, 1994). Education plays a key role in continuation to research and development via interactive learning, which, in turn, promotes growth of output and total factor productivity. Of course, this depends upon the way of financing it (Schaper, 2003).

Again, economists like Cornia and Stewart (1995), Muysken *et al.* (2003) developed a model explaining the optimal expenditure on health and consumption by adding a health accumulation function to the Cass-Koopmans optimal growth model. They suggest that a healthy population contributes more to growth than a fast growing capital stock. Of course, physical capital and quality of labour are complementary rather than substitute.

In point of fact, it is pertinent to note that in some studies like the one made by a Nigerian economist, while studying empirically the direction of causality between defence expenditure and human capital expenditure, by employing Augmented Dicky Fuller and Phillip Perron tests during 1970-2000, the crowding out effect of defence expenditure on education and health is not that simplistic (Adebiye, 2005). There are varieties of channels through which defence expenditure or debt service obligations may have an impact on the stock and quality of human capital. Some of the channels may ultimately be of a positive nature. Defence expenditure may impart technical training in military services, augmenting skill content of the existing labour force and help dismantle social rigidities by virtue of the fact that it is a progressive institution. It is sometime perceived to promote a civilised society which, in turn, dispenses with feudal and social obligations towards market obligations towards a market oriented capitalist system which places a much greater premium on enhancing the quality of human capital. Improving quality of the labour force yields implicit, non-economic outputs related to the generation of ideas and decision which have a significantly positive impact on investment, innovation and other growth opportunities (Roux, 1994).

2. It is true that as per the UNDP Report on Human Development, India has achieved a commendable progress in many areas of human development[1]. Famines and starvation have been virtually eliminated; life expectancy has almost doubled from 32.01 years in 1951 to 63 years in 2001. A similar rate of progress has been achieved in reducing infant mortality which has been halved from 146 to 74 deaths per 1,000 live births between 1951 and 1995. Even more remarkable has been the achievement in improving literacy which has increased from 18 to 52 per cent between 1951 and 1991.

Unfortunately, the data are somewhat misleading. For instance, the Census reveals that the absolute number of illiterates actually increased between1980 and 1991 although there was a reduction in the rate of literacy. Gender and spatial disparities in literacy are also very high. Only 30 per cent of rural females are really literate in 1991. Educational surveys also reveal that one in three children do not attend schools. Dropout rates are absolutely high with 35 per cent of children leaving schools before completing primary schools. The proportion of underweight children under five years is still as high as 60 per cent and the provision of health care facilities is woefully inadequate. One in four births is not attended by health personnel. The deficiency of facilities is particularly acute in rural areas. Roughly, one in five persons in the rural areas neither drinks safe water nor has access to health care facilities. Even, the aggregate figures conceal more than reveal state of affairs (Datta, 1997).

Certain important peculiarities are in order. In the first place, there are significant variations in the quality of life across regions and across categories of people. For instance, the infant mortality rate in Orissa was as high as 124 in 1991 or about 80 per cent higher than the average in India. There can be, again, a large variation within the same state. Orissa is an example of the phenomenon. Ganjam district recorded an infant mortality rate of 164 per 1,000 live births[2].

India's performance in improving the quality of life of the average Indian has to be evaluated in relation to the success achieved by other countries at a comparable stage of development. India's performance has been at best mediocre. The average India's life expectancy or the Indian infant mortality rate today is comparable to that in South Korea or Thailand in 1960. As far as adult literacy rate is concerned, the Indian achievement in 1992 is significantly lower than that of these countries in1970. The average citizen in South Korea or Thailand was more educated and in much better health than the average Indian today even before these countries enjoyed much economic success[3].

A highly developed and vibrant North-East India with strong integrative ties with the mainstream India in terms of social, political and economic justification is necessary for the stability and supremacy of India as another rising power in South Asia. A failure to recognize it will make India politically and strategically vulnerable in the long run.

Economic performances of the North East Indian States are in general dismal. However, Assam, for instance, has the lowest growth rate in Net State Domestic Product (NSDP)—3.31 per cent per annum during 1980-81 to 1999-2000; whereas, all India growth rate is 5.1 per cent during the same period. Arunachal and Mizoram's growth rates are 8.12 and 8.31 per cent per annum respectively. Growth rates of per capita NSDP are at lower in almost all other states. This is mainly due to a very high population growth, much above 2 per cent per annum as against the national average growth rate of 1.81 per annum. In almost all the states, the performance of North East Indian States is worse than the all India average. The manufacturing sector is growing only at 2.3 per cent per annum, while the all India average is 6.4 per cent (1980-2001).

The Human Development Report (2003) prepared by National Council of Applied Economic Research under the sponsorship of United Nations Development Programme stated that while identifying the significant gap between urban and rural areas in human development, education, health and other welfare services were heavily concentrated in the urban areas. The incidence of rural poverty is quite high. More than 39 per cent of the rural population was living below the poverty line. Even in the case of literacy, rural urban disparities, inter-district variation and dropout rates in schools were spectacularly evident. Except Manipur, the dropout rate in schools exceeds 60 per cent. Even with regard to the health sector, a wide inter-state disparity was conspicuous by their presence. Mizoram had just a single nurse for every 22,000 persons; it was 5,330 persons in the case of Assam. Contrary to popular perception, the status of women in the region was far from being in an equal footing with that of man.

In fact, North East India has still a long way to go as far as Human Development is concerned.

The allocation of health in developing countries in general is much lower than that of developed countries. Public expenditure on health in Canada and Sweden are at similar levels with respect to their ratio of GDP. It hovered around 7 per cent of GDP. This allocation is higher than that of other developed countries. It should be noted that Canada has a predominantly publicly financed, privately delivered health care system. Among the developing countries, India's public expenditure on health is as low as less than one per cent of GDP which is lower than that of Bangladesh, Pakistan, China and Sri Lanka. The public health expenditure in India is mainly spent on the communicable disease control programms, family welfare schemes and nutrition schemes. Sri Lanka's social indicators are quite high in relation to income. It threw a hypothesis that social spending can have an impact on improvements in social indicators. At the same time, Pakistan's social indicators are by any standard poor, specially taking care of relatively rapid income growth (Tables 3.1 and 3.2).

India showed a better status in relation to the public expenditure on education at around 3 per cent of GDP. This is higher than many other developing countries like Indonesia, Sri Lanka, Pakistan and China.

It is true that growth of per capita income, while important, is not the primary determinant of improvement in human development. Hence, there is a need to understand the effectiveness of public policy intervention *versus* 'growth mediated human development'.

3. To examine the impact of social sector public expenditure on human development indicators across countries, a fixed effects models of pooled least squares for the early 1990s is employed. The model is specified as follows:

$$HDI_{it} = \alpha + \beta PUB + \chi PCs + \mu$$

Where, HDI_{it}: Human Development Index

α_i : country-specific intercepts

PUB_{it} : Per capita combined expenditure on education and health in US $.

PC_{it} : Per capita income in US $

Table 3.1: Public Expenditure on Health of Selected Developed and Developing Countries

Country	*1993*	*1994*	*1995*
Canada	7.34	7.05	6.70
Australia	5.66	5.64	5.65
Bangladesh	1.13	1.16	1.15
China	2.05	2.06	1.92
India	0.71	0.69	0.65
Indonesia	0.67	0.66	0.63
Malaysia	1.45	1.31	1.26
Norway	6.71	6.62	6.66
Sri Lanka	1.41	1.59	1.64
Sweden	7.66	7.39	7.08
United Kingdom	5.85	5.81	5.83
United States	6.08	6.29	6.47
Gambia, The	1.83	1.81	1.72
Pakistan	0.98	0.96	1.02
Korea, Republic	2.06	2.01	2.14

Source: World Development Indicator Database, ADB, 1999.

Table 3.2: Public Expenditure on Education of Selected Developed and Developing Countries

Country	*1993*	*1994*	*1995*
Canada	7.22	6.91	—
Australia	5.56	5.38	5.45
Bangladesh	—	—	—
China	1.86	2.40	2.27
India	3.58	3.54	3.31
Indonesia	1.78	1.42	1.40
Malaysia	5.15	5.18	4.68
Norway	8.17	8.25	8.08
Sri Lanka	3.14	3.20	3.04
Sweden	—	7.96	8.07
United Kingdom	5.48	5.42	5.33
United States	5.26	5.36	—
Gambia, The	5.06	5.35	5.61
Pakistan	2.60	2.79	2.80
Korea, Republic	4.43	3.70	3.68

Source: Same as in Table 3.1.

It is evident from the estimates (Table 3.3) that an increase in public expenditure on human resource development by 1.000 US dollars could increase the HDI to 0.5 purchase points. The co-efficient of per capita income is 0.019. that is, a rise in per capita income by

1000 US dollar in a country can lead to 0.019 percentage point rise in HDI. Spending on social sectors has stronger impact on human development than economic growth per se (Chakrabarty, 2003). Public expenditure on human capital formation gets transformed to the end results of better human development indicators. The public policy stance plays a crucial role in human development.

Table 3.3: Effects of Public Expenditure on Education and Health and Per Capita Income on HDI: Fixed Effects Models

Variable	*Coeficient*	*Std Error*	*t-Statistics*	*Probe*
Per capita Income	0.01	0.005	3.74	0.0009
Pub Exp on H & E	0.50	0.058	8.63	0.0
CAN-C	-405.05			
AUS-C	-348.59			
BAN-C	-6.85			
IND-C	-11.83			
INDO-C	-21.90			
KOR-C	-261.38			
USA-C	-405.92			
UK-C	-335.79			
NOR-C	-841.32			
GAM-C	-12.96			
PAK-C	-12.88			
SRI-C	-17.79			
SWE-C	-570.78			
MAL-C	-134.45			
CHIN-C	-9.48			
Adjusted R^2	0.99			

Source: Reproduced from Chakrabarty: Public Expenditure and Human Development, 2003.

The justification for higher public spending on education is generally based upon its impact on individual's life-time income (i.e. the social rate of return). Again, the emphasis on health care is justified on the ground that it ameliorates the impact of diseases on the productive life years of the population. These might be the compelling reasons for shifting the public resources towards education and health care. For example, a 5 percentage point increase in the share of outlays for primary and secondary education increases gross secondary enrolment by one percentage point. A similar increase in the share of primary health care spending can decrease infant mortality rates by 2.3 (per 1,000 live births) and child mortality rates by 4.9, per 1,000 children under 5 years of age (Gupta, 1999). Of course, the performance in these sectors is also dependent on the capital income, urbanization and illiteracy, access to safe sanitation and water etc. There are also some other important determinants like private sector spending.

However, if expenditure allocation on these sectors boosts economic growth and promote the well-being of the poor, care should be taken to their size and efficiency. It is pertinent to note that shifting allocation within the sectors does matter. Shifting spending towards primary education has a positive impact on enrolment rates and student persistence; shifting spending towards primary health care has a reasonable impact on infant and child mortality.

4. Hence, there is a need for generating a right kind of prioritization by way of allocation of funds through public policy stance[4]. Well-prioritized supportive social sectors expenditure that could be combined with reasonably good distribution of income and moderate growth rate would be precisely effective in generating appropriate consistent human development. This reprioritization would lead the states to a better macro-economic future, through improvement in key areas.

Here is the case for state intervention for reprioritization. In fact, the case for state intervention in public expenditure stems from market failure. The operation of the market may not necessarily, by itself, activate the signalling response and mobilization of economic agents to achieve efficiency in both static (allocative efficiency) and dynamic (shift in the production functions) terms. This may be for different reasons. For example, market cannot determine the prices of the public goods since all goods and services are not traded. Again, in view of existence of externalities, a difference between market price and social value may exist. And there may exist some kind of moral hazards because of information asymmetry between the providers and the consumers of services. The case for public expenditure proceeds from market failure of one kind or another. Hence, the need for state intervention in response of proper allocation of expenditure on some key areas. The case for concern towards public policy intervention in providing human development reflects the community's growing concern with social aspects of development. The so-called soft sectors like education or health occupy the center stage. The key issue is: in India, what kind of scope is there for reallocating public expenditure at the state level.

Human development sectors often overlap with the social sectors. They are primarily in the domain of the states, as per the constitutional assignment in India. The states have certain obligations and limitations in its operational behaviour. They have certain challenges to break the vicious circle of poverty, low level of human development and low income. There are a lot of budgetary constraints like infeasibility on the part of the states to vigorously push public expenditure financed by deficiency and consequent borrowings, committed expenditure of some sort or the other like salaries, interest payments, loan repayments etc. on the part of the states.

In India, the allocation of the funds within the social sector is not optimal[5]. A sizable proportion of the funds is absorbed by staffing costs. This leaves very little for capital investments and maintenance of infrastructure. The pattern of social sector spending also reveals an anti-poor bias. For instance, while the bulk of the poor live in the rural areas, a large chunk of public expenditure on health is spent on urban hospitals which provide curative health care. The state of many primary schools is abysmal with a dearth of teachers as well as teaching aids, although higher education is heavily subsidized. There are also glaring anomalies in local authority budget allocations with amusement parks and water fountains seeming to get priority over sanitation and water supply.

5. The debate on the role of the state as an important service provider is quite pervasive since Adam Smith. But the proper measurement of the public sector performance, particularly social sector priority is limited. The measurement issue is to be considered in terms of efficiency measurements. It compares resources used to provide certain services, the inputs with outputs. Efficiency frontiers could be constructed and therefore inefficient situations can be detected. So, it implies the possibility of a better performance without increasing allocated resources[6].

There are also some other points which should be taken care of. While reprioritizing, it is not fair to assume that each of the sectors is independent of the other. There is certain degree of complementarity's between different sectors like health and physical infrastructure. As an example, the operation of x-ray machine calls for a provision of electric power supply. The methodology should be broadened to capture the cross effects. Again, certain parts of the public expenditure may be pre-determined. Hence, the method of re-prioritization is to be applied to the total expenditure minus non-negotiable components.

NOTES

1. As per the latest Human Development Report, India has a rank of 126 out of the total of 177 countries. However, there are ten countries, including Vietnam and Mongolia, which have a per capita income of less than India, but have a higher Human Development Index. In all these countries, the per capita public expenditure on health is two to three times than of India (at 88 PPP $). Again, there are 51 countries with a Human Development Index value less than that of India. Almost all of them also have a GDP per capita also lower than India. However, when it comes to adult literacy, for which data are available for only 37 countries, there are 15 countries that have adult literacy rates higher than India. The list includes the poorest countries of South East Asia like Myanmar, Cambodia and Laos. The persistence of these different forms of deprivations and the absence of a level playing field call for a right kind of paradigm for inclusive growth and development. The state have their legitimate roles to play (Kannan, 2007).
2. Ghana allocates an average of 20 per cent of its total expenditure to education yearly. Between 1986 and 1992, Botswana spent 21 per cent of her expenditure on education, Malaysia 19 per cent, Kenya 20 per cent, Uganda 15 per cent.
3. India's social record looks impressive until we look at the regional variations and compare with other countries. Although deprivation in health and education in Sub-Saharan Africa is comparable to India, we may soon fall behind even these countries.
4. Of course, there is an increasing awareness of the need to re-orient priorities. This is particularly reflected in the composition of Government expenditure on health, communicable diseases control programmes, family welfare schemes, nutrition programmes, etc. Operation Blackboard demonstrates the same shift in the allocation of education expenditure.
5. Even as there has been marked improvement in the fiscal performance of most of the states during 2006-07, the expenditure on social sector, specially health and education leaves a lot to be desired. Social sector spending by all states which stood at 38.6 per cent of total expenditure in 1990-95 declined to 36 per cent in 2007-08.
6. Economists generally employ Data Envelopment Analysis in what concerns the evaluation of result robustness.

REFERENCES

Adebiye, M. A. (2002): *Public Expenditure and Human Capital in Nigeria: An Auto Regressive Model* (Unpublished).

Bhaskar, Dutta (1997): Taking a Poor View of the Human Development, in *The Telegraph*, Calcutta, August 21.

Chakrabarty, S. (2003): *Public Expenditure and Human Development: An Empirical Investigations*, Working Paper, NIPFP.

Gupta, S. *et al.* (1999): *Does Higher Government Spending Buy Better Results in Education and Health Care*, IMF Staff working paper, February.

Kannan, K. P. (2007): Interrogating Inclusive Growth: Some Reflections; *Indian Journal of Labour Economics*, Vol. 50, No. 1, pp. 17-30.

Roux, Andre (1994): Defence, Human Capital and Economic Development in South Africa, *African Defence Review*, No. 19.

Sen, T. and K. Karmakar: Reprioritization of Public Expenditure for Human Development (Unpublished Paper).

4

Sustainable Human Development and Accelerating Economic Growth

P. K. CHAUBEY

Introduction

It is interesting to note that the first of the series of the HDR Reports started out with the requiem for pursuit of economic growth, denouncing the use of GDP/GNP as indicators of human progress—which were based on commodity approach and promoted instead what came to be known as capability approach and devised, howsoever defective, a measure of human progress with the name of Human Development Index. The Report cleverly portrayed the cumulative rankings of 130 countries according to human development index and GNP per capita in the same graph, showing a concave curve for HDI and a convex one for GNP per capita and thus impressing upon to focus on the UNDP endeavours on human development, human development index and perhaps capability approach. There is a lot of tricksters involved in such depictions, yet people got swayed by some of the stories that were brought to buttress the shift in focus in development debate particularly among economists.

The Report 1990 was able to impress upon that many countries with modest GNP per capita, like Sri Lanka, Chile, Jamaica, Costa Rica, Tanzania and Thailand, have been able to fare better in terms of human development dimensions while many other countries with high GNP per capita like Oman, Gabon, Saudi Arabia, Algeria, Mauritania, Senegal and Cameroon did not do so well. What Saudi Arabia could not achieve at income *x*, Brazil achieved at one-third of *x*, though both were far behind in human development indicators.

The message to convey was that gap between countries in terms of GDP per capita may keep widening and yet there exists scope for closing the gap in terms of human outcomes with regard to health reflected in life expectancy and infant mortality and education and literacy. It was indeed suggested that public policies designed at meso level—across-the-board variety like immunisation and primary education and targeted variety like food stamp and supplementary feeding programmes—can do wonders even if a country is not able to affect a sustained course of growth with distributive justice.

However, there has been a quiet reversal surprisingly almost right from the beginning and revival for reliance, in due course, on economic growth. While it is generally argued in the Report of 1990 that a dozen of war guns could not be equivalent to a hundred of tonnes of milk, which measures like GNP readily accept, as a critique of commodity approach and measurement in terms of GDP/GNP, the Chapter 3 of the Report 1990 proposes that *if human development has to be durable it must continuously be nourished by economic growth*. It verily says that 'excessive emphasis on either economic growth or human development will lead to developmental imbalances that, in due course, will hamper further progress'. Progress of what is not explained.

While we are today talking of sustainable development, taking care of depleting non-renewable natural resources, restraining degradations of renewable resources and pollution of human environment, we are also talking about accelerating growth rate, which has been pretty high, much beyond ever achieved in history, for quite a foreseeable future. That ever since the Second World War and liberation from foreign yoke the developing countries have been seeking unabated acceleration in growth rate, which has generally taken place and of late to begin with the countries of moderate size and later the countries of huge numbers have succeeded in pushing the growth trajectory itself upward. As a consequence growth of the world GDP has also accelerated. The issue whether the idea of accelerating growth is compatible with sustainable development and at that sustainable human development, has not been adequately addressed.

We propose to discuss in the following sections the issues of steady growth and stable development, environmental sustainability and economic growth, and sustainable development and sustainability of human development, in that order.

Steady Growth and Stable Development

Though many people define development as both process and product (level), we find it extremely difficult to digest. So we take growth as process and development as level in this piece.

We have all grown up understanding properties of steady growth, which if stable, will continue for ever, or at least indefinitely as well as what happens if there is a slip from the path of steady growth. The level of development will therefore keep rising *pari passu* without let up should growth rate remain steady and exceeds growth rate of population. But we have also been learning that countries after countries always wanted to plan for accelerating growth. Ignoring exceptions, in each plan we in India have been planning for a growth rate which is higher than that stipulated in the preceding plan. Sometimes we succeeded and on other occasions we failed. But in each perspective-plan exercise, we built such models in the planning exercises as to leave the stock of capital at the end of the plan, which would sustain still higher growth rate in post-plan period.

So, in a way, we all yearned, as did others, for ever-increasing, accelerating growth rate. GDP, in terms of which growth rate is measured, would however take care of depreciation of man-made capital stock but avoid taking notice of degradation and depletion of natural stocks, or, for that matter, harmful consequences of producing commodities called goods, in terms of their twins bads. Many attempts to adjust GDP for environmental damage and for accounting for loss of leisure have not yielded encouraging results. Now the attempt is to green GDP accounts by preparing satellite accounts.

Since the Report of the Club of Rome, viz., *Limits to Growth* and contemporaneous UN Conference on Human Environment in Stockholm in early 1970s, various countries by and large noticed the problems associated with the development paradigm pursued by the West and to be pursued by others. In view of the exposure to the West of the elite in the developing world and inadequacies of goods and deficiencies of services in comparison with the West we continued and propose to continue to pursue a high and rising rate of growth with the hope that it will relieve us of our pressing problems of poverty, ignorance and squalor. We turn blind eye to the harmful consequences at present, if they really loom large, with the hope that they could well be taken care of later when we have resources to spare for tackling them. As we cannot wait for clean technologies to be developed at home and we cannot afford to import them from abroad, we are psychologically adjusted to attach low social cost to externalities that affect us in terms of health, hygiene and sanitation. The question is whether proposition of accelerating growth is compatible with sustainable development in terms of ethics and environment if growth itself causes both inequity in social fabric and degradation of natural resources.

Those who have come to suggest an alternative approach to view the development and advised to concentrate on human outcomes in terms of capabilities 'to be' and 'to do' and so meticulously distinguished between 'being well' and 'being well off', could not finally move away from suggesting that growth is the necessary condition. The position that growth is not a necessary condition but policies are, has itself transformed over years into one in which growth is not a sufficient condition but a necessary one for advancing the level of human development and sustaining it.

Sustainability of development would then mean dynamic stability of level and therefore of the system. In the older terminology it is static equilibrium in the sense that all flows, in and out, in the system are constant and therefore, the stocks are also constant. And hopefully it is ensured that so-called renewable stocks are not exploited beyond their renewal rate and pushed into non-renewal category.

Steady growth would keep on raising the level but accelerating growth would raise it at an increasing rate. If they do not cause problem then *development path may still be called stable*. Will that be depends on technology, resources and population. But can we really have such a stable development path *ad infinitum*? This means we can never think that our wants can ever be satiable. We are no doubt an acquisitive society but must we remain ever greedy? Or can we also develop a notion of standard of living, with which we feel we are happy?

Environmental Sustainability and Economic Growth

Economic growth has now been considered as not being so much of intrinsic importance but for having instrumental value for human development as it provides for higher quantum of resources to carry out policies and programmes which directly improve the level of human development. Some have also thought of engendering it with equity concerns by suggesting what has come to be known as pro-poor growth. They have also cautioned to make prudent use of natural resources and keeping environment clean so that our future generations do not suffer for our follies.

These 'normative' prescriptions had their counterpart in empirical laws. For example, Kuznets suggested that as a society develops, to begin with, inequality also increases but there comes a level where after it starts declining. This is known as Kuznets inverted-U-curve. From experiences of many countries one may perhaps verify the law. Kuznets did not suggest how long does it take to cross the hump and whether it will vary with growth trajectory, or according to nature of the State or from culture to culture. He also did not disentangle the contribution of policies pursued to the end of justice or to the end of growth, as if we live in world of complete *laissez faire*.

Following Kuznets' thesis regarding growth-inequality relationship, it has been argued that there exists an inverted-U-curve relationship between level of development and the level of environmental ambience. It has been argued that with rise in income people will demand to begin with goods and services in higher quantities causing higher level of pollution, but after reaching a certain level of consumption of conventional goods and services they would opt for better quality of environment for living, working and lazing. There would be resources available to develop or import clean technology for production and people will pay for keeping environment clean. From experience of many European countries we gather the impression that they have been able to improve their natural environment after passing through a phase of bad, suffocating, dirty environment, which was an important consequence of industrial revolution. Today many of them have cleaner technology of production and provision and cleaner environment for living, working and lazing. Yet, the most important and powerful country is shirking from committing to do much say in the matter of climate change.

Taking a cue from theory of demographic transition, which starts from a low level of growth, transits through phases of high, explosive growth and levels at low level of growth again. In the same vein we can think of environmental transition from a low level of pollution (pristine natural environment) to another low level of pollution after passing through the phase of high level of pollution and problems associated with that. But let us note an important difference. As there is difference between pre-transition low population growth and post-transition low population growth, there is difference between pre-transition low level of pollution and post-transition high level of pollution. The difference is that age-structure of pre-transition population is different than that of the post-transition population. While in the former it is low life expectancy and median age, in the latter life expectancy and median age are higher. Similarly, pre-transition low level of pollution will be at low level of living while low level of post-transition pollution would be at a high level of living. That can be an optimistic way of looking at the prospects emerging on the horizon.

Sustainable Development and Sustainability of Human Development

Both the themes, viz. sustainable development and sustainable human development have been perused and pursued in the Human Development Reports. So we feel obliged to devote the final section on these two themes and the linkages between them.

Dictionary meaning of sustainability is about holding up; bearing; supporting; providing for; maintaining; sanctioning; supporting the life of. Does nature sustain itself, maintaining the balance? May be, but human beings in practically all societies did not accept the natural course of the nature. They intervened with application of their intellect in modifying its processes in order to improve their conditions and conditions of their progeny. Using this approach which is anthropocentric/anthropogenic, not holistic in view of some philosophers, Gro Harlem Bruntland defined sustainable development in the report of the World Commission on Development and Environment "Our Common Future": *Sustainable development is development that meets the needs of the present without compromising the needs of future generations to meet their own needs.* Development in this context is a deliberate attempt by human beings. It has, therefore, to be only Pareto-improvement kind in the intergenerational context, as some scholars have put.

The very notion of sustainable development puts a condition on our deliberate efforts that they do not compromise the needs of future generations. On the one hand it seems to suggest a variety of development, which does not promote such growth which as goes beyond environmental carrying capacity, on the other it addresses to inter-generational equity question in a unique manner. To translate the Harlem's idea in the parlance of economics would mean: no less enjoyment for future generations than that for the present generation. If more, how much more? Therefore, conversely speaking, it should also imply no less enjoyment for the present generation. In the limit it would mean enjoyment of generation G_{t+1} should be the same as that of generation G_t. The position goes a little beyond Pareto-optimum because here we are putting a normative context. In Pareto optimum we are not comparing the levels because interpersonal, and by extension inter-generational, comparisons are not permitted in Pareto framework. No doubt, we can see that the above definition does not expressly compare the needs of various generations.

There are then issues of defining the needs. Shall they be the same as of the present generation? Has it been ever so? Shall each generation have the same set of needs and of the same intensity? At any given juncture, who will decide the needs of the future generation? By counterfactual reasoning, a generation can decide in its own estimate about the needs of the next generation or next few generations but not all next generations. They can perhaps at best be the aspirations of a generation for its succeeding generation(s).

Conclusion

In a perceptive note on "Intergenerational Equity, yes—but what about inequity today", Robert Solow in one of the Human Development Reports holds that the concept sounds nice and says it is nice to think that our endeavours to improve our living should not be allowed to lead to a poorer life for descendents. Then he asks: why should not we think of intra-generational equity between nations and regions, why not between different classes and divisions?

Let us for a while think, as to why the idea of sustainability was so easily accepted in comparison to the idea of equality. This comes naturally and very well nurtured culturally that we care more for son than for brother, that we care more for daughter than for sister, and that we care more for children than for spouse. There is something instinctive in our breast that we easily jump to accept such notions without analyzing its implications. Emotional takes, it seems, over the rational.

We hardly realize in this kind of discourse that it is the intra-generational inequities, which perpetuate and accentuate, if not attenuated, over time. Taking care of intra-generational equity would automatically lead to inter-generational equity as the former would moderate the consumption vector also. The issue thus boils down to equitable consumption and sustainable consumption.

Finally, sustainable human development means what? Reading literally, it implies that health and education status and opportunities for work and leisure ought to be no worse, possibly better for our children and their children. They might not exactly translate in terms of indices life expectancy, literacy and security or in terms of cooperation, participation. Longevity, literacy or securities are not intrinsic in themselves. They are so in a societal context. But there is no doubt that the notion of human development, which is by far more individualistic in approach, has to be so oriented as to reflect communitarian concerns.

5

Climate Change and Human Development: HDR 2007/2008

RAJ KUMAR SEN

The annual Human Development Reports (HDRs), in addition to presenting data on various human development indices, always focus on a relevant issue with global bearing on human development. The focal theme of the Human Development Report 2007/2008 is 'Fighting Climate Change: Human Solidarity in a Divided World' as climate change due to global warming is now internationally considered to be one of the most important and complex challenges facing humanity in the present century. For a large section of the humanity damaging climate change is now either an imminent threat or a current reality. This includes vulnerable groups and localities like the pastoralists, rain-fed farmers in arid and drought-prone areas, localities prone to frequent floods and natural disasters, small island states, river deltas and others. The linkages between climate change and human development raise important questions about social justice and cross-generational equity, which have called for a wide-ranging policy dialogue about social discounting, the pricing of carbon, the distribution of responsibilities for decarbonising global economic growth and others. This Report aims to explore the ways in which the climate change will lead to increased vulnerability, hold back poverty reduction, widen inequalities based on gender, region, income and ecological degradation and therefore, will roll back human development undermining international cooperation aimed at achieving the Millennium Development Goals (MDGs).

The Report is also highlighting the implications of growing inequalities in recent years in terms of carbon emission in particular and in terms of level of living in general among the developed and developing countries and regions in general. This is also true in the area of their capabilities to face the challenges of climate change leading to unprecedented reversals in human development for a large section of the world population. As some damaging climate changes are now inevitable, it is necessary to device ways for their adaptation with greater resilience. It has been also noticed that, while the world's poorest countries and their poorest people bear little responsibility for the built-up of carbon-dioxide and other global warming gases in the earth's atmosphere, they stand to bear the major brunt of the social and economic consequences. It is expected that this feature will reinforce the case for action by highlighting the consequences of failure for the world's poor. The HDR has focused on the following four broad clusters: (i) Climate change impacts and adaptation with implications for human development and the MDGs, (ii) Living within a carbon budget and the agenda for mitigation, (iii) The Kyoto Protocol and beyond; and (iv) Statistical measurement of the impacts which is quite inadequate at present. The present paper has discussed all these issues from the viewpoint of the developing countries in general and from Indian standpoint in particular. It has demonstrated the limitations of a forestation policies for carbon trading for reducing global warming. It has also emphasized on the urgent need to control inequalities on every front within tolerable limits. Moreover, emphasis on demand management of energy requirements of the future, need for research for commercial use of alternative clean sources of energy (but not nuclear power) at the national and international levels, united action to press for a sustainable and environment-friendly consumption pattern and development of a reliable environmental data base, are among the other issues highlighted in this paper. It is organized as follows: Section I—Introduction; Section II—Climate Change Impacts and Human Development and the MDGs; Section III—Living within a carbon budget and Agenda for mitigation; Section IV—The Kyoto Protocol and Beyond; Section V—Statistical measurement of the impact; Section VI—Conclusions and Suggestions.

I. Introduction

In the closing decades of the 20th century, scientists often predicted that wars will be fought in the 21st century on the issue of command over water. Even the focal theme of the HDR 2006 was *'Beyond*

Scarcity: Power, Poverty and the Global Water Crisis'. But within a few years after the beginning of the current century, the course of events took such a different turn that at present the world is deeply engrossed with another severe atmospheric problem, i.e., the problem of climate change originated from the long-term event of global warming. In fact, the year 2007 has played a historical role in pushing the problem of global warming to the forefront as before 2007 almost nobody gave due importance to this problem and many world leaders following US President Bush often slighted the environmentalists as if they are making a mountain out of a mole hill. In fact US did not sign the Kyoto Protocol which may be considered as the most effective weapon to fight against the problem of global warming. But things started to change rapidly with the beginning of the year 2007 when the first draft of the IPCC IVth Assessment Report was published in February and the final Report came to the public in the month of May. The draft report itself may be considered as the first document which categorically mentioned about the grave dangers of global warming and the urgent need to control it. In fact before this report, scientists not only visualized this new danger, but also some debated about the future prospect, viz., whether the world is heading towards global warming or global cooling. This report initially created stir among the EU countries and rapidly other countries joined in their reaction against global warming. For the first time in the world, UK enacted legislations based on the Kyoto Protocol. Germany led the EU towards a more strict environmental policy. The final report only confirmed the draft with more empirical evidences about the dangers of global warming. These include melting of the polar ice leading to the rise of the sea level and consequent permanent submergence of many islands and ingress of the sea water to the low coastal areas in the equatorial region. This was followed by the UN meeting at Geneva where pressure was mounted on US, the largest polluting country of the world, to take steps to control the emission of green house gases (including mainly CO_2, methane and other gases like nitrogen oxide, and others) causing global warming. Though USA did not agree to bind itself by any deadline or level of green house emissions, yet they declared to find solutions to global warming in their own way. This shows that USA, who did not sign the Kyoto Protocol and remained quite indifferent about the environmental problems, had to soften their stand about global warming as a consequence of the international pressure. In October, the IPCC itself and the former US

Vice-President Al Gore, a noted environmentalist shared the Nobel Prize for peace, which sent according to the Nobel committee itself, a clear political message to highlight the problem of global warming in the world's political economy. Within a couple of weeks the UN published another similar report—Global Environment Outlook IV. This report was more specific and stronger in recommendations to mitigate the problems of the climate change than its predecessor, IPCC IV report. According to this report the current development process that we are following is unsustainable. It is well-known that growth means disequilibrium but there is a tendency in the nature to restore the equilibrium automatically. But if this disequilibrium is carried too far, then it becomes difficult to achieve a new equilibrium. The present society is depleting the natural resources at a rate which is estimated to be nearly 25 per cent higher than that critical limit. The degree of unsustainability is therefore becoming unbearable everyday. The solution to this situation hence lies in making our development process sustainable by changing our life-style and obviously the contours of the present development paradigm. The solution to the problem of global warming lies through a sustainable development process.

At this juncture the UNDP published its annual Human Development Report (HDR). We are aware that the HDRs, in addition to presenting data on various human development indicators, always focus on a relevant issue having global bearing on human development. In November 2007, when the concept note on the HDR 2007 was published, its focal theme turned out to be *'Climate Change and Human Development—Rising to the Challenge'*, which again highlighted the issue of the dangers of the adverse climate change through global warming. But a couple of months later when the Report was finally published, a slight change in the Report was noted; it was termed as the HDR 2007/2008 and the focal theme became *'Fighting Climate Change: Human Solidarity in a Divided World'*. The theme of course remained identical with a minor difference in emphasis. It emphasized on four broad clusters of issues. These are: (a) Climate change impacts and Adaptation—Implications for Human Development and Millennium Development Goals (MDGs), (b) Living within a Carbon Budget—The Agenda for Mitigation, (c) The Kyoto Protocol and beyond: the World after 2012, (d) Statistical Measurement of the Impact. This paper will discuss all these aspects in the following sections before we reach our conclusions and make policy prescriptions at the end.

However, the linkage between 2007 and renewed emphasis on global warming did not end with the publication of the HDR. In Bali, Indonesia the global meet on environment was held during December 3-14 which was extended by one day as no unanimity was reached until December 14 on the question of the direction of the global environment policy after the end of the Kyoto Protocol in 2012 which was the main objective of holding the Bali Summit. The US declined to sign the 'compromised text' which invited sharp reaction from others who demanded that either US must give the leadership or it must quit. This attitude brought change in the stand of the US and the Summit ended not with a failure. The G-8 countries (US, Japan, Germany, Britain, France, Italy, Canada, Russia), pledging to move towards a low carbon society, have now agreed to cut carbon emissions in half by 2050. However, they did not specify whether the starting point would be current levels or 1990 levels, and refused to set a short term target for reducing the emission of green house gases. However, the present non-binding nature of the agreement was considered as a step towards a binding international treaty to be negotiated in Copenhagen in 2009. However, this declaration came under severe criticism from environmentalists, who called it a missed opportunity and said it ignores the urgent need to cut emissions more rapidly as according to one source, we have to reduce 80 to 90 per cent from current levels to avoid the worst impacts of climate change. The Group of Five (G-5) leaders (India, China, Brazil, Mexico and South Africa), under growing pressure from the G-8 nations to join global efforts to combat climate change, said that it is essential that developed countries take the lead in achieving ambitious and absolute GHG emissions reductions of 25 to 40 per cent of the 1990 level by 2020. They also urged on the international community, particularly developed countries, to promote sustainable consumption patterns and lifestyles responsive to climate change mitigation requirements. India believes that the primary responsibility for the current state of the climate lies with developed countries. India's per capita emission of CO_2 is 1.2 tonne, a fraction of figures for the US, Japan or UK. The IPCC head Pachauri said that the developed countries should get off the backs of India and China and should help them move towards a low carbon economy with technology and finance.

II. Climate Change Impacts, Human Development and the MDGs

The HDR 2007/2008 in its Foreword by the Executive Director, UNEP, has claimed that climate change is now a scientifically established fact in spite of the lot of uncertainty about the exact and predictable impact of GHG emissions. At least it can be said that the climate change due to GHG emissions is not reversible in the foreseeable future and the heat trapping gases sent to the atmosphere will stay there for more than 100 years. The climate change is different and more difficult than other policy challenges as our activities in this context will affect not only our lives but also the lives of our children and grandchildren to a larger degree. The risks of climate change are also well-known like the melting of ice on the north and south poles which can place many islands and coastal areas under water and bring drastic climatic changes affecting large section of the vulnerable people in many fragile regions of the world. Such dangers are increasing with everyday of inaction. As the world is a heterogeneous place with people having widely unequal income and wealth, the impact of climate change will affect different people and different regions very differently. For a large section of the humanity, damaging climate change is either an imminent threat or a current reality. Increase droughts, extreme weather events, tropical storms, sea level rises and unforeseen natural events like these will affect adversely mainly large parts of Africa, many small island states and low coastal zones perhaps within a few decades. In fact, the poorest and most vulnerable communities around the world have already started to feel the impact of the climate change. They include, for instance, the pastoralists, rain-fed farmers in arid and drought-prone areas, people living in localities prone to flood and disaster-prone areas like river deltas and small islands, etc. In a macro aggregative sense, such damages may not be large in the short term, but from a micro and localized standpoint the losses are really enormous. This non-uniform distribution of costs from the climate change, at least in the short and medium term, makes the policy challenges most difficult. And such difficulties are accelerated due to the fact that those who have largely caused the problem of the GHG emission, the rich countries, are not going to be the sufferers. On the other hand the poor countries and the poor people are the most vulnerable ones who do not contribute to such emissions significantly.

In the long-run, of course, the climate change is a real threat to human development as the development progress of many countries is increasingly being hindered by the climate change impacts which also undermine the efforts of the international bodies to reduce extreme poverty. The HDR likes to correlate the efforts to fight the impacts of climate change with the fight against poverty and other human vulnerabilities as included in the UN 2000 Millennium Development Goals (MDGs). It states that climate change will be one of the defining forces to draw the human development scenario during the 21st century in spite of the many uncertainties associated with the impact of the climate change, there is no doubt that the effects of global warming can be expected to magnify the existing disadvantages. Thus despite high rate of economic growth across much of Asia, most countries are off-track for realizing the MDG targets for halving extreme poverty and deprivation in 2015. The case of India is particularly highlighted as an illustration. It has been observed that the recent 'emergence of India as a high-growth economy, with per capita incomes rising at an average of 4-5 per cent since the mid-1990s, has created enormous opportunities for accelerated human development.' But at the same time, this rapid economic growth has produced modest progress in poverty reduction and nutrition. Most developing regions are reducing poverty at a slow pace and the MDG target is likely to be missed by approximately 380 million people. Both South Asia and Sub-Saharan Africa are unlikely to achieve MDG target of halving under-nutrition by 2015. Nearly half of the rural children are underweight for their age and this has not reduced perceptively since 1992. Similarly, the MDG target of a two-thirds reduction in child mortality by 2015 is likely to be achieved by only 32 out of 147 countries monitored by the World Bank and this will result in 4.4 million additional deaths by 2015. All these deficits on account of achieving MDGs point to the deep and widening inequalities across the world. The Sub-Saharan Africa will account for almost one-third of world poverty in 2015, up from one-fifth in 1990. Income inequality within countries is also rising and today more than 80 per cent of the world population live in countries with widening income differentials.

The state of the world's environment provides a vital link between human development and climate change. The UN in 2005 has referred to the global deterioration of vital ecosystems (like mangrove swamps, wetlands, forests, etc.) which are highly vulnerable to climate change just like the people who depend on them. In fact in India the major share of poverty is primarily due to ecological poverty as most of the rural poor (including tribal and forest people) are dependent on natural resources for their livelihoods. With time, the incremental risks created by climate change intensify and the prospects for sustained human development after the 2015 target year for the MDGs are directly threatened. As per the IPCC IV Report, this will be accompanied with loss of bio-diversity and increase in the national disasters. Various surveys conducted in this context show (Nicholas, 2006) energy generation through fossil fuel consumption is the largest source of emission of greenhouse gases, accounting for 61 per cent of the sources, followed by deforestation (18%) and agriculture (14%). In 2002, US topped the list of per capita CO_2 emission with a value of 20.1 metric tonne of CO_2 (mainly due to their unsustainable life style and consumption pattern and their unwillingness to sacrifice even a little for the sake of the world), while the values for China and India are respectively 2.7 and 1.2 only. This shows that high income countries of the world are mainly responsible for GHG emission for their addiction to oil consumption (in preference to other renewable sources of energy) but the poor countries are to bear the major brunt of its impact due to their comparative lack of capacity in terms of technology and infrastructure to protect themselves from natural hazards though recently US and her allies have become vocal against China and India for their increasing contribution to GHG emission resulted from their high rate of economic growth in recent decades. Of course, it has been also pointed out that all such conclusions are based on a few sample surveys conducted in high income countries only and that too by some NGOs only and not by any official research institute. There may be some commercial interests also behind such conclusions popularized by such agencies. It has been pointed out by the meteorological department of Kolkata that in the winter of 2005-06, the temperature of Kolkata was normal or less than that for most of the days. However, in the northern India there are some instances of global warming but in southern India the situation is completely the opposite and this may be actually termed as an incidence of global cooling. These scientists also questioned about the methodology of recording the temperature in particular areas as it will depend upon the location of the monitoring station. They also denied the possibility of submergence of the different areas of the world in the near future.

The HDR in this context has also identified five human development 'tipping points'. These are: (a) Reduced agricuitural productivity, (b) Heightened water security, (c) Increased exposure to coastal flooding and extreme weather events, (d) The collapse of ecosystems, and (e) Increased health risks. It has been estimated that the climate change effects on human development on these counts will be: (i) an additional 600 million people facing acute malnutrition by the 2080s; (ii) an increase by 2080 in the number of people facing water scarcity by 1.8 billion; (iii) an increase in the number of people experiencing coastal flooding by between 180 and 230 millions; (iv) adverse effect on the people dependent upon fish for their livelihoods and nutrition; and (v) an additional 220-400 million people could be at increased risk of malaria. All these five indicators of human development reversals, due to climate change impacts, are sources of disempowerment for the poorest section of humanity numbering close to 2.6 billion people.

III. Living within a Carbon Budget and Agenda for Mitigation

From the HDR it is now clear that there is now near unanimity about the increase in the global warming and about its adverse impacts on the present and the future generations. It is further agreed that the current emission rate of CO_2 is unsustainable for the future unless we adopt appropriate steps to control it. However, there is a basic difference between the views of the developed North and developing South as the South believes that unless the rich countries reduce their fossil fuel consumption, living within a carbon budget is not possible. But the North is totally against reducing their oil energy consumption and disagrees with the South about their responsibility for global warming. In fact they want to blame the industrial activities of the newly emerging high growth economies like China and India for increasing carbon concentration in the atmosphere. Even when they agree to join the international efforts to decarbonise the atmosphere up to a tolerable limit (currently the target being 450 ppm CO2e), they try to devise various other ways to reduce CO_2 emission. Accordingly, they are emphasizing on afforestation to absorb CO_2 and other GHGs through methods like carbon trading and/or creation of carbon sinks in the developing countries of Asia, Africa and Latin America. However, this emphasis on afforestation is basically wrong as deforestation accounts for a minor share (18%) only of carbon emission while the major factors like energy consumption (61%) are not taken care of. Besides there is also very scanty proof of the capacity of forests about CO_2 absorption in order to effectively curb the adverse effects of global warming. The HDR also indirectly and sometimes directly favoured carbon trading and carbon pricing as the essence of mitigation policy which will be more market dependent rather than bringing back bureaucratic controls in the form of quotas. Let us discuss the issues of carbon trading and creation of carbon sinks briefly.

The Kyoto Protocol, formulated in 1997 and implemented since February 2005 by 84 countries first formulated a method to convert all GHGs into CO_2 equivalent and thus converted it into a trading commodity. Like all other trades, this carbon trade also follows all kinds of commercial rules including taxes, exchange rates, etc. The signing countries are divided into two groups: List 1 consisting of EU and other countries for whom there is fixed scale for reduction of GHGs and the remaining countries for whom there is no such limit. Now the second group of countries may trade with their excess carbon quota. The Protocol has also specified three mechanisms for carbon trading, viz., Clean Development Mechanism (CDM), Joint Implementation (JI) and Emission Trading (ET), respectively explained in paragraphs 6, 12 and 17. It has also introduced the concept of carbon saving for list one countries (i.e., the rich ones), with the help of which they can avoid the controls fixed on their carbon emission activities. In 2006, the price of CO2e was 5 to 16 US$ and there was trading of carbon savings to the extent of 22 bn $ within first 9 months of 2006. With the current international agenda for mitigation of global warming through carbon trading, may be considered as not only a recipe to continue the present unsustainable consumption levels of the rich, but also that at the cost of the poor. The main reasons for such comments are: complex and debatable methodology of carbon trading, scope of polluting countries belonging to list one to continue their activities in the name of investment in other countries violating the rules of environment security, and others with complete reliance on free trade helping to the growth of profit for the mega industrial concerns. Carbon trading is also intimately connected with SEZ and production of bio-fuels which are in many cases objectionable from the point of South as the first involves a compromise with the nation's sovereignty coupled with extreme exploitation of labour, while the other often leads to lack of food security as vast food growing areas of land are transferred for the cultivation of vegetables producing bio-fuels.

Equally objectionable from the view point of the developing countries is the policy towards the construction of carbon sinks in developing countries. According to this policy, the rich countries can earn the right of establishing polluting industries by helping afforestation in the third world countries. This is unacceptable to such countries for reasons more than one. The creation of carbon sink lead to blocking vast areas of land for a very long period under new forest for the purpose of absorption of GHGs from the atmosphere thus preventing the concerned country from using the land from any industrial or other developmental activity which she may require in future. Already the land acquisition process has started in countries from Guatemala to Uganda, from Brazil to Sri Lanka, from Ecuador to Indonesia and similar other countries of the South. As an illustration it may be cited that Norway has established a gas fuelled power generation centre by Naturekraft and Industrikraft Midtnorge Corporation. As a compensation for the resulting carbon emission they have contracted the government of Uganda through an organization engaged in afforestation to acquire 5160 ha of land at a minimum price for 50 years to plant pine and eucalyptus trees. Such projects are rightly called colonialism by the rich countries. The theory of global atmosphere, where carbon absorption in one region can compensate the carbon emission in another far away country is seriously flawed as environment and atmosphere are not only heterogeneous but also they are region and season specific. The equation between afforestation and carbon absorption without consideration of the special geo-physical features of the different parts of the world is, to say the least, is over simplistic and hence unacceptable. A better option would be reforestation of the degraded forests with eco-friendly trees, which will restore the benefits of forests on the one hand helping the eco-system and will not lead to any loss of scarce land in a densely populated country like India.

IV. The Kyoto Protocol and Beyond

We have already noted that though the Kyoto Protocol has floated new ideas to control carbon emission, they are mostly framed to help the rich countries placing the burden of reducing emission on the poor countries mainly. Besides such methods like carbon trading, carbon sink and carbon savings are all highlighting on afforestation as the main policy to control global warming. Even in this situation, the US, the most carbon emitting country of the world, has refused to sign this Protocol with the consequences of undermining its importance and making it partly ineffective. Moreover by allowing the pollution of air to continue through carbon trading, it is difficult to understand how carbon trading may be considered as a CDM. Even the scientists of the high income economies are doubtful about the efficacy of the carbon trading to control global warming as this is derived from economic theory initially conceptualized by Ronald Coase and further propagated by J.H. Dales and UN Environment Protection Agency. But this is supported by only a small amount of empirical evidence from US practice untested in the various economies in which the mechanism must work. The IPCC Report could not mention clearly that in order to control and reduce global warming the present pattern of development and the inherent philosophy of continuously increasing consumption need to be changed without any further delay even when they are aware that the main factor global warming is high and increasing rate of fossil fuel consumption and the onus mainly lies on the high income countries of the world. In fact the western economies and in particular the US are consuming the world resources at a much higher rate than their low income neighbours in the South and they are not at all ready to reduce their consumption as according to them the basis of rationality for a consumer is to maximize his utility through consumption of more and more commodities and services and that for the producers is to maximize their profit from production without having any regard either for the protection of the nature or humanity especially when they belong to low income economies. This strategy directly goes against the Gandhian concept of sustainable consumption. It was correctly said by this man of foresight that the world has enough to meet our needs but not so to meet our greeds. The mad race for increasing the level of living in line with the western culture by the developing countries is also self-defeating as they do not have the military and economic control over the world resources which was enjoyed by the colonial powers during their initial phase of industrialization nearly two centuries ago. This has been pointed out even by the HDR. Mahatma Gandhi once reflected on how many planets might be needed if India were to follow Britain's pattern of industrialization. The Report has estimated that if all of the world's people generated GHGs at the same rate as some developed countries, we would need nine planets!

We may conclude this section with some comments on the recent upsurge in favour of the nuclear power as a source of clean energy in the context of the demand to reduce fossil fuel consumption as it leads to global warming, though there were very few takers of the nuclear energy in the 80s and 90s of the last century when the fallout from the nuclear accidents like Chernobyl disaster was fresh in memory. It is argued that nuclear power, which is already providing in 2003 around 16 per cent of the world's electricity, is the most promising and viable alternative. These contentions are really misleading as nuclear power contributes to only 6 per cent of the marketed fuel sources of which electricity is only one form of energy. Moreover, unlike other sources of energy, nuclear power is not suited to multiple modes of energy uses. Since, then, the total energy use has increased significantly although nuclear electricity output has gone up only marginally. In a study by Mycle Schneider and Antony Froggatt *(The World Nuclear Industry Status Report)* in 2004, it has been shown that considering the average lifetime of 40 years per reactor, a total of 280 units would have to be replaced over the next 20 years, which means a decline of nuclear plants operating in the world considering huge capital, technical and organizational challenge needed to establish new nuclear plants. This is further corroborated by the 2007 data of the International Atomic Energy Agency and the World Nuclear Association, the most respectable pro-nuclear sources, we may expect a massive shortfall as compared to the existing installed capacity even in the best case scenario. Further barring China, Russia and India, no other country seems to be adding to the efforts to lead the so-called 'nuclear renaissance' to stem the tide of nuclear decline, making it difficult to understand how nuclear can be taken as a serious fossil fuel alternative. In spite of these revealing facts, the US has projected a 31 per cent rise in the nuclear energy output in 2030 over the 2003 level. But the forecast for the total energy output for the same period has been a rise of 70 per cent leading to a decline of nuclear's share to less than 5 per cent only. Thus how nuclear energy can help reduction of GHGs which will go up by leaps and bounds under the present global scenario. This is a feature in spite of the tremendous investment of the OECD countries that goes into nuclear energy research, a total of 50 per cent of the energy research budget while only 8 per cent goes into research in renewable energy resources. In India also, the nuclear industry has been favoured in a similar manner, as the 2006-07 budget allocated Rs. 603.64 crore under the Ministry of Non-conventional Energy Sources while the allotment under the nuclear energy research programme was as much as Rs. 5505.08 crore. In spite of this criminal neglect, the growth of wind and solar energies since the last two decades really brings hope as the emerging sources of clean power in the near future.

Finally, it should also be remembered that the nuclear power is not also so clean as propagated by its supporters. Barring the fission stage, which is only one part of the whole nuclear fuel cycle, the mining, processing and reactor construction, lead to increase in green house pollution. The nuclear plants are known to produce radioactivity released into air during their everyday routine operation. Besides, there are the threats of nuclear accidents (most of which are suppressed), terrorist attacks and nuclear proliferation. But the most important danger of nuclear power is the problem of disposal of nuclear waste, the annual production of which from a typical nuclear reactor is 25-30 tonnes of spent fuel. Till today there is no satisfactory solution for dealing with high level radioactive waste. Already many countries of Africa are used as dumping grounds of such dangerous wastes from the rich North. Now they are eyeing the Asian continent to discover new dumping grounds for such activities...

V. Statistical Measurement of the Impact

It goes without saying that without proper and precise measurement of the climate change impact, it is not possible for the states to adopt effective policies to mitigate the impact. At the same time it is also true that a reliable data base for environmental resources neither exists nor is there any serious attempt to build it up rapidly in a systematic and reliable manner following the state-of-the-art methodology as far as possible. At present we have the data on climate change estimated from a few field surveys conducted mainly in rich countries only. However, such results cannot be universal considering the localized and heterogeneous character of the environment. The climate change impact is also dependent on a region's environment and its adaptation capability.

However, the most serious problem in the impact measurement problem is the politics involved in it as the MNCs try to influence the empirical results. It may be mentioned that since 1985 the current research on carbon trading is being conducted by the MNCs and their funded organizations like World Meteorological Organization, International Panel on Climate Change, etc., instead of UN sponsored research by independent environmental economists. Naturally such institutes and organizations are preparing their reports in the line of the demands made by high income countries of the world. These countries are now demanding the right of industrial pollution in exchange of their aid towards afforestation in low income economies which will help in absorption of CO_2. The IPCC has in fact conceded such atrocious demands and for doing so they have deviated from all sorts of valuation techniques to measure the carbon absorption capacity of the forests. They are totally silent about the feasibility of compensating industrial pollution through afforestation and consequent carbon absorption. In many cases the MNC-funded organizations could purchase important personalities in the movement against global warming. For instance, the lawyer James Cameron, one of the main founders of the Kyoto Protocol has been appointed as Vice-Chairman of a bank called Climate Change Capital associated with carbon trading. Similarly, chief of the UN Green House Gas Emission Trading, Frank Jassua has joined as a director of Natsource, which is one of the leading corporate houses engaged in carbon trading in USA. It is also observed that the Green Peace, one of the front runners in opposing the corporate dominance in environmental issues, has silently accepted the blanket approval of carbon trading in the name of Clean Development Mechanism. The NGOs like World Resource Institute of Washington, World Business Council for Sustainable Development, World Wide Fund for Nature and others are continuously trying to establish the right for carbon trading. All these amply indicate towards a biased assessment of the extent of climate change impacts and efficacy of the mitigation strategies.

VI. Conclusions and Suggestions

It is obvious from the analysis of the previous sections that while the climate change impacts are discussed in details by the HDR 2007/2008, the causes of such impacts are not analysed properly. Even the impacts are presumed on the basis of scattered analysis mostly done in the rich countries and such conclusions are really difficult to apply for the poor South. So far as the mitigation policies are concerned the only emphasis given is on afforestation neglecting more important causes like CO_2 emission due to use of energy based on fossil fuel consumption by the rich countries in an unsustainable manner. It appears that in the name of carbon trading and creation of carbon sinks based on questionable assumption of a homogeneous world atmosphere, the North is trying to control the South on the plea of mitigating the global warming without sacrificing their own over consumptive life-style.

However, the criticisms levelled against the North do not mean that the South has nothing to do to mitigate the impacts of climate change. In fact the rich and elite class of such countries is contributing to global warming by consumption of fossil fuels which is no less than that of the high income economies of the world. Further, the governments of such economies including India are following the same type of development paradigm which is mainly responsible for the global warming and there is also no serious attempt to control the steeply rising demand for the energy consumption based on fossil fuel or for any effective substitution by energy based on non-conventional sources (solar, wind, agricultural waste, etc., but not nuclear power as it is neither clean, nor safe and not adequate as explained above in Section IV). This indicates that the developing countries should set on the one hand their own house in order by adopting appropriate steps even in the face of steep opposition from the groups with vested interest and on the other should negotiate with the low income economies to put a united opposition to the North to compel them to cartel their unsustainable consumption levels and use of fossil fuel so that the global warming may be checked under the present unipolar world order. It is of course obvious that such strategies are extremely difficult to get implemented unless the present conventional development paradigm is changed.

On the front of afforestation, India should give priority to reforestation of degraded forests and try to keep her forest cover in different regions at their respective optimum levels as there should not be any uniform norm of forest cover in our mega-biodiversity country of continental dimensions. At the same time she need not be cowed down by the pressure of the MNCs to develop carbon sinks in this highly populated country whether further reduction of arable land may lead to the loss of food security. This has already been demonstrated in different regions of India by popular protest against acquisition of agricultural land for the creation of new industries and Special Economic Zones. Afforestation is good for environment but not so when it is done by external pressure and jeopardizes the food security of the common people. This is true not only for India but also for all highly populated large economies of the world governed by popular democracy.

It appears that developed world is keen to keep the developing South as the perennial source for the supply of raw materials and other resources for their industrialization process to continue uninterruptedly. Thus in 1995, the export of raw materials from Latin America to Europe and USA has gone up by 245 per cent compared with 1980 and this percentage is further increasing. This shows that the interest of the high income economies lies in keeping the rate of modernization and industrialization of the developing world at a low level.

Acknowledgements

I am thankful to Sri Somnath Hazra for his assistance in the preparation of this paper. However, the usual disclaimer applies.

REFERENCES

Adve, N. (2007): Implications of Climate Panel Report, *EPW*, March 24.

Agarwal, Anil (2000): *Climate Change: A Challenge to India's Economy*. Centre for Science and Environment, New Delhi.

Chacraverti, Santanu (2007): *Nuclear Power: A Treacherous Choice.* DISHA, Kolkata.

Hazra, S. and R.K.Sen (2008): 'Globalization, Deforestation and Global Warming.' CD containing Papers accepted for the 15th World Congress of the International Economic Association, Istanbul and published by Turkish Economic Association, Ankara, Turkey.

IPCC (2007): Contribution of Working Group II to the Fourth Assessment Report of the Intergovernmental Panel on Climate Change.

Jacob, J. (2005): Forestry and Plantations: Opportunities under Kyoto Protocol. *EPW*, May 14.

Meena, Om Prakash *et al.* (2005): 'Global Warming and its Impact on Agriculture.' *Kurukshetra*, Vol. 53, No. 8, June.

Nicholas, S. (2006): 'What is Economics of Climate Change?' *World Economics*, Vol. 7, No. 2, April-January.

Sen, Raj Kumar and Somnath Hazra (2008): 'Global Warming, Deforestation and India.' K.K. Roychoudhuri and P. Dutta (eds) *Global Warming.* D.N. College, Aurangabad, West Bengal.

UNDP (2007): *Human Development Report 2007/2008*. Palgrave Macmillan, New York.

Section Three

Regional Dimensions of Economic Development

6

Inter-District Variations in the Level of Human Development in Assam

NIRANJAN ROY

Introduction

Geographically the State of Assam is comprised of three physical divisions, viz., the Brahmaputra Valley, the Barak Valley and the Hill Range. The Brahmaputra Valley comprising the northern part is largest in terms of both area and population. The Barak Valley in the south is separated from the Brahmaputra Valley by the Hill Range of Karbi-Anglong and North Cachar Hills in the middle. The population of the state as per 2001 census is 26.64 million, of which 13.78 million are men and 12.85 million are women, the sex ratio being 932. The trend in population growth shows that the decadal variation in the state has been very much larger than in the country as a whole almost in all the decades. It is only in the last decade that the decadal variation has declined to a rate less than that of India. There are 23 districts in the state including two hills districts. About 12 per cent of the population of the state lived in urban areas in 2001. It indicates that the state is still much less urbanized than most states in the country. It is still an overwhelmingly rural society. In this case also there is large inter-district variation.

About 70 per cent of the people of the State still dependent on agriculture. In the agriculture sector, the overall growth rates has been stagnant and as such it could generate sufficient surplus for investment or create purchasing power in the rural sector to provide a market for local industries. Cropping intensities and crop productivities remain low. The small size and fragmentation of holdings, low irrigation coverage and the limited use of modern technologies and practices are some of the constraints in the agricultural sector. Despite having potentialities industrial diversification and growth has been constrained by the inadequacy and quality of infrastructure, geographical isolation and lack of well developed markets. The age old tea industry has been facing crisis over the last few years.

Growing unemployment has been a serious cause of concern. About 45 per cent of the rural people live Below the Poverty Line. The infrastructure development in the state has been extremely low.

The position of Assam in the human development perspective in the national level is not impressive. The state rank among the 15 countries in 1991 was 10 which came down to 14 in 2001. The Assam Human Development Report 2003 provides a benchmark for assessment of the status for each district in the state. There are wide variations in all the indicators of HDI among the districts.

Economic Growth, Human Development and Public Expenditure

The "human development" has come to be accepted in the development economics literature as an expansion of human capabilities, a widening of choices, an enhancement of freedoms and a fulfilment of human rights. Rising incomes and expanding outputs, in the human development framework, are seen as the means and not the ends of development. Indeed, defining people's well-being as the end of development and treating economic growth as a means have been central messages of the annual Human Development Reports published since 1990 (Sakiko and Shiva Kumar, 2003). Conceptualised and initially articulated by UNDP's (United Nations Development Programme) first Human Development Report in 1990, this is a perception that has grown into a global objective and a shared vision. UNDP stressed that the real wealth of a country is its people and the purpose of development is to create an enabling environment for them to enjoy long, creative and healthy lives. In fact HDI (Human Development Index) is a summary measure of human development. It measures the average achievements in a country in three basic dimensions of human development: (a) A long and healthy life, as measured by life expectancy at birth; (b) Knowledge, as measured by the adult literacy rate (with two-thirds weight) and the combined primary, secondary and tertiary gross enrolment ratio (with one-third weight); (c) A decent standard of living, as measured by NSDP (Assam Human Development Report, 2003).

Economic growth can have a positive impact on human development through an increase in general level of per capita income, poverty reduction and higher public expenditure on education, health and related sectors (Ghosh, 2006). Economic growth by increasing the revenue base of the economy may enable the state to spend more on social sector. The country like Sri Lanka achieved relatively higher human development despite being a developing country. The countries achievement in this respect is supported by high level of public expenditure on social sector (Dreze and Sen, 1989).

Thus one of the significant policy initiatives towards reducing inequalities has been increasing public social sector expenditure. The Government of India both at the Centre and the States has been taking primary responsibility of social sector expenditure since independence. The county's social sector expenditure averaged 5.8 per cent of GDP during 1990s but declined marginally during the current decade. The total expenditure, as ratio to GDP, averaged 16.5 per cent during 1990s and increased thereafter. Fiscal priority to social sector defined as the ratio of Social Sector Expenditure (SSE) to total expenditure, on an average, has been nearly 37 per cent during 1990s. This ratio has shown a declining trend since 1998-99 to reach 27.9 per cent in 2004-05. However, there is little consensus in the literature regarding the optimum size of SSE in an economy. It depends, *inter alia*, on the level of human development population and the stage of the development of social infrastructure. Nevertheless, UNDP in its Human Development Report (1991) provides minimum target expenditure ratios (minimum target for total expenditure to GDP is 0.25, SSE to total expenditure is 0.4, expenditure on basic social services to SSE 0.5 and expenditure on basic social services to GDP is 0.05) related to social sector which is expected to benefit the human development aspect in an economy. Notwithstanding, the robustness of such targets, a comparison of these targets shows the level of SSE is comparatively low in India (RBI, 2006).

Status of Human Development in India

Following the UNDP's human development framework, the National Human Development Report in India seeks to put together indicators and composite indices to evaluate development process. A State level database has been put together covering around 70 distinct indicators, in most cases, in terms of gender and rural-urban break up and presented in over 150 tables. This has prompted an extensive use of Census of India data. In addition, data from alternative sources, including the NSSO, NFHS and other official and some independent sources has also been used. The HDI has been estimated for all the States/Union Territories, separately for rural and urban areas, for early eighties, using data covering the period 1981 to 1983; for the early nineties, covering the period 1991 to 1993 and in case of selected major states for the year 2001, using the data for the period 1999-2001 (NHDR, 2001). The details of HDI for India since 1980s are depicted in Table 6.1.

Table 6.1: HDI for India

States/UTs	*1981 Value*	*1981 Rank*	*1991 Value*	*1991 Rank*	*2001 Value*	*2001 Rank*
Andhra Pradesh	0.298	9	0.377	9	0.416	10
Assam	0.272	10	0.348	10	0.386	14
Bihar	0.237	15	0.308	15	0.367	—
Gujarat	0.360	4	0.431	6	0.479	6
Haryana	0.360	5	0.443	5	0.509	5
Karnataka	0.346	6	0.412	7	0.478	7
Kerala	0.500	1	0.591	1	0.638	1
Madya Pradesh	0.245	14	0.328	13	0.394	12
Maharashtra	0.363	3	0.452	4	0.523	4
Orissa	0.267	11	0.345	12	0.404	11
Punjab	0.411	2	0.475	2	0.537	2
Rajasthan	0.256	12	0.347	11	0.424	9
Tamil Nadu	0.343	7	0.466	3	0.531	3
Uttar Pradesh	0.255	13	0.314	14	0.388	13
West Bengal	0.305	8	0.404	8	0.472	8
All India	**0.302**		**0.381**		**0.472**	

Source: NHDR, 2001.

At the national level, HDI, which takes a value between 0 and 1, has improved from 0.263 in 1981 to 0.381 in 1991 and to 0.472 in 2001. The HDI in 2001 varies between 0.638 in case of Kerala and 0.365 in case of Bihar. Among the better-off States, Punjab, Tamil Nadu and Maharashtra had a HDI value of above 0.52. On the other hand, Uttar Pradesh, Assam and Madya Pradesh had values less than 0.400. Assam could maintain its same position, that is, rank 10 during the period 1981 and 1991 but dropped to 14 in 2001. The disparities between the rural and urban attainments in Assam continues to be quite high.

Human Development Scenario in Assam

The Assam Human Development Report, 2003 provides a basis for assessment of the present status of different districts in regard to the important components of Human Development Index. The HDI for the state and the corresponding indices for the districts have been calculated on the basis of the latest available data for the year 2001. The HDI as calculated for different districts is shown in Table 6.2. The results of Table 6.2 have been analysed using statistical tools and reported in Table 6.3.

Some of the important findings derived from Table 6.2 and the statistical analysis reported in Table 6.3 are:

1. There are significant variations in the state across districts in human development. Only seven districts have HDI value higher than state average indicating considerable inequity among the districts. The difference between lowest and highest value of HDI is around three times. Most of the upper Assam districts have HDI values higher than state average and all the lower Assam districts have lower values. To determine whether there are any impact of decadal variation of population on HDI between upper and lower Assam, the population data of the decades 1941-51, 1951-61 and 1991-2001 have been taken into consideration. This is shown in Fig. 6.1. Traditionally the lower Assam districts have higher growth rate of population than the upper Assam. The apparent explanation for this higher growth rate of lower Assam districts is that these districts had to bear the blunt of partition related migration of refugees from East Bengal (now Bangladesh) to a great extent than the upper Assam (Dass, 1980). In the post-independence period also the state of Assam has been having a higher rate of growth of population than India as a whole. However, for the first time in 2001 Census the decadal growth rate (1991-2001) in Assam appears to be less than that of India as a whole.

Table 6.2: Human Development Indicators for Different Districts of Assam Ranked by HDI Value

Rank/District	*HDI Value*	*Income Index*	*Education Index*	*Health Index*
1. Jorhat	0.650	0.564	0.722	0.664
2. Kamrup	0.574	0.573	0.701	0.450
3. Golaghat	0.540	0.409	0.650	0.564
4. Karbi Anglong	0.494	0.491	0.535	0.457
5. Morigaon	0.494	0.562	0.551	0.371
6. Dibrugarh	0.483	0.162	0.654	0.636
7. Sibsagar	0.469	0.242	0.702	0.464
Assam	**0.407**	**0.286**	**0.595**	**0.343**
8. Cachar	0.402	0.266	0.634	0.307
9. Barpeta	0.396	0.385	0.527	0.279
10. Tinsukia	0.377	0.082	0.571	0.479
11. Hailakandi	0.363	0.234	0.563	0.293
12. N.C. Hills	0.363	0.211	0.650	0.229
13. Sonitpur	0.357	0.071	0.552	0.450
14. Nagaon	0.356	0.179	0.583	0.307
15. Kokrajhar	0.354	0.145	0.474	0.443
16. Nalbari	0.343	0.076	0.641	0.314
17. Lakhimpur	0.337	0.154	0.657	0.200
18. Goalpara	0.308	0.146	0.536	0.243
19. Karimganj	0.301	0.078	0.620	0.207
20. Dhemaji	0.277	0.026	0.622	0.186
21. Bongaigaon	0.263	0.103	0.557	0.129
22. Darrang	0.259	0.057	0.514	0.207
23. Dhubri	0.214	0.102	0.454	0.086

Source: Assam Human Development Report, 2003.

Table 6.3: Descriptive Statistics of Human Development Indicators for Different Districts of Assam

	HDI	*Income Index*	*Education Index*	*Health Index*
Mean	.3902	.2351	.5943	.3463
Std. Deviation	.10924	.17522	.07290	.15729
CV	28.0	74.53	12.27	45.42
Variance	.01193	.03070	.00532	.02474
Range	.44	.55	.27	.58
Minimum	.21	.03	.45	.09
Maximum	.65	.57	.72	.66

2. Among the Income, Education and Health indexes, the values of income index are more heterogeneous and more variable than other two. The income index is much skewed. Only six districts have income index values higher than state average. As such there is a wide variation among the districts in regard

to the income and there is an around 75 per cent variation in this respect.

3. In regard to the Education Index though 11 districts have higher values than the state average but the values of the districts are less variable and more homogeneous than both Health and Income Indexes. Thus in regard to the educational attainments there is no evidence of wide disparity among the districts. Again in attaining the overall value of HDI (0.407) for the state as a whole, the value of Education Index (0.595) contributed much. Thus among the different components of HDI the state has attained significant achievement in the sphere of education.
4. In regard to the Health Index 10 districts have higher values than the state average. In this case also there is wide variation to the extent of around 45 per cent among the districts. The difference between minimum and maximum value, i.e., 0.58 indicates considerable in equity in this respect. The district-wise variations of HDI and its three components are shown in Fig. 6.2.

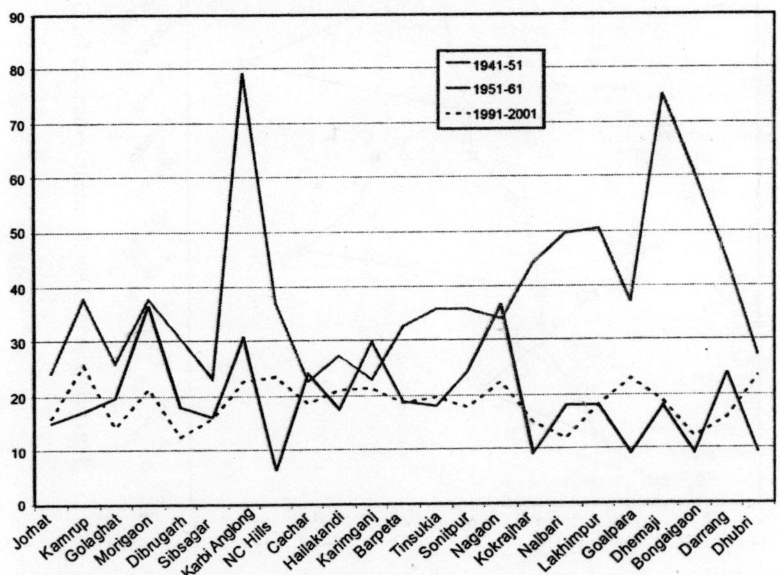

Fig. 6.1: Decadal Variation of Population in Different Districts of Assam, 1941-51, 1951-61 and 1991-2001

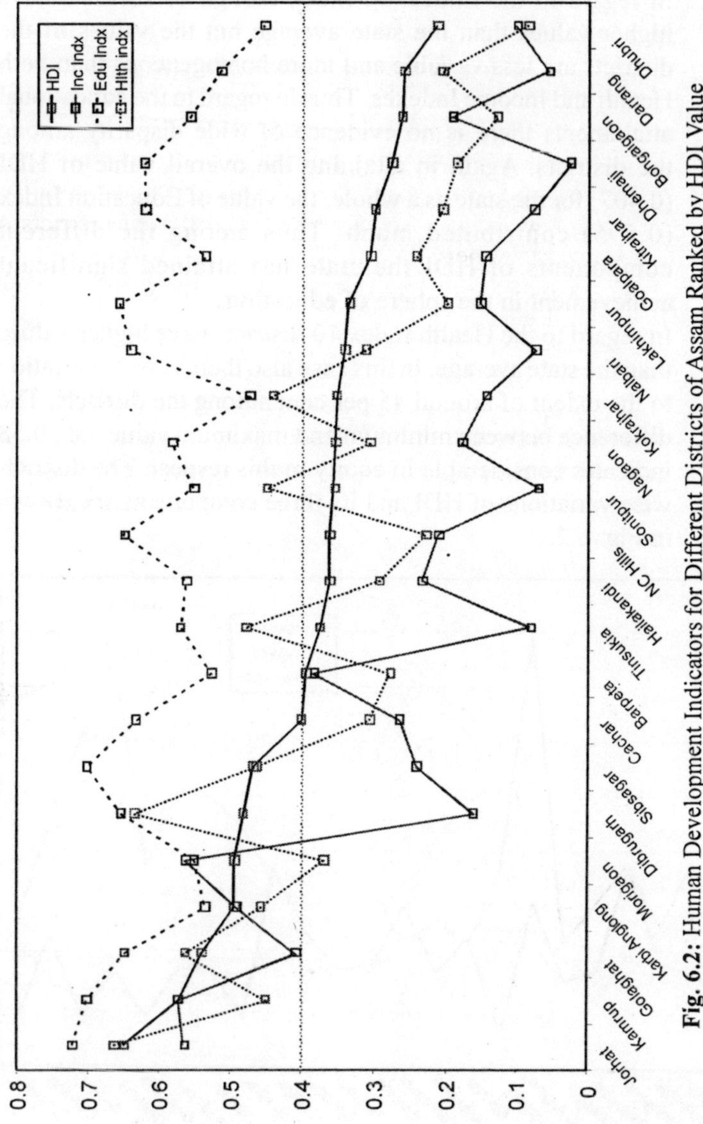

Fig. 6.2: Human Development Indicators for Different Districts of Assam Ranked by HDI Value

To find out the factors associated with significant variations across districts of the state related to HDI a regression equation 6.1 has been specified and parameters were estimated using OLS method. The results as obtained are shown in Table 6.4.

$$\mathbf{HDI_i = \alpha + \beta_1 UP + \beta_2 LR_i + \beta_3 SR_i + \beta_4 HB_i + \beta_5 DP_i + U_i,}$$
$$i = 1, 2 \ldots 23 \qquad \ldots\ldots \mathbf{6.1}$$

Where

HDI = Human Development Index for different districts of Assam as per Report of 2003
UP = Percentage of urban population in the districts as per 2001 census
LR = Percentage of literate population in the districts as per 2001 census
SR = Sex ratio in the districts as per 2001 census
HB = Availability of hospital beds per 100 population
DP = Per capita district domestic product for the year 1994-95
α and β's are parameters to be estimated
U = Random disturbance term.

The results of regression analysis are given in Table 6.4.

Table 6.4: The Results Least Square Estimation for Explaining Variations in HDI Across Districts

Variables	*Coefficients Beta*	*Std. Error*	*t-statistics*
Constant	4.147	2.121	1.955*
UP	-0.001867	0.005	-.411
LR	0.007158	0.003	2.446*
SR	-0.004334	0.002	-2.036*
HB	0.239	0.760	.314
DP	0.0001017	0.0001	-1.462

F = 3.964**
$R^2 = 0.538$
*, ** indicates significant at .05 and .01 level respectively

Results and Discussion

The R^2 value -0.538 indicates that the model gives a good fit to the sample data. Moreover two variables and the constant term comes out to be statistically significant. The F-statistics for over-all regression is also highly statistically significant. Thus on the whole, results obtained from the analysis are fairly robust and credible.

The coefficients of the variables LR and SR comes out statistically significant. The positive and significant coefficient of the variable LR indicates that literacy has contributed to a greater extent in human development in all the districts in the State. The coefficient of the variable SR is statistically significant and negative. This confirms gender disparities and as such women population in the State are at disadvantaged position and lag behind men in all aspects. The coefficients of other variables UP, HB and DP do not come out statistically significant.

Human Development and Gender Gap in Assam

The statistical analysis confirms continuing inequities confronting women in the State. The differences are in educational attainments, measured by literacy rates and school enrolment figures; in the share of income earned measured by Female Work Participation Rate (FWPR) and proportional rate of female wages to male wages. Other gaps are in the health status of males and females measured by life expectancy at birth and infant mortality rates. Although, the origin of much of this discrimination lies deep in societal structures, the processes of modernization and change have accentuated inequity. The neglect of women's health, denying women equal access to family and community resources such as food, education, health care and income and the devaluation of women's work and overall dignity as persons, all contribute to gender discrimination (AHDR, 2003). Shivakumar (1996) observed the fact that overall progress and prosperity in terms of HDI does not necessarily mean equal and good position of women. The Gender Related Development Index (GDI) shows wide variations across districts in the state and the values varies between 0.012 to 0.0877. The difference in HDI and GDI indicates the extent of gender disparity in a particular district. While the positive difference between HDI and GDI indicates greater gender inequity, the negative difference implies comparatively better position in terms of HDI. The 12 districts in the state falls in the first category and the rest 11 districts shows negative differences (refer Fig. 6.3 and Table 6.5).

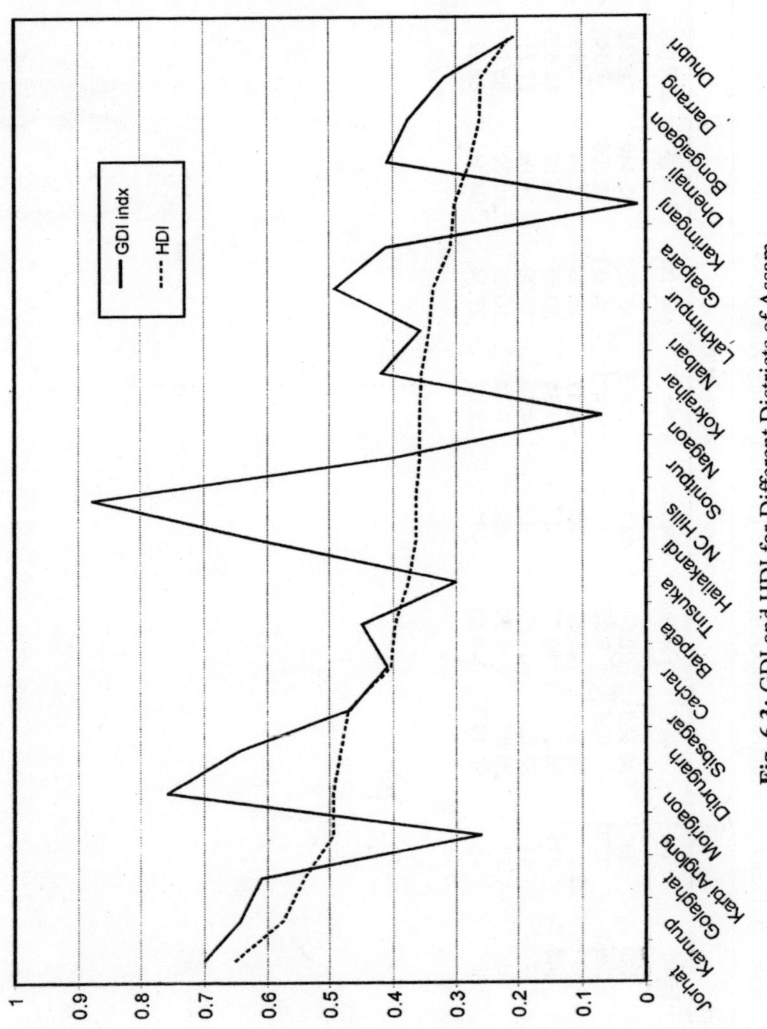

Fig. 6.3: GDI and HDI for Different Districts of Assam

Table 6.5: Descriptive Statistics on GDI, HDI, WPR and Literacy Rate Across Districts in Assam

			Work Participation Rate							
	GDI	*HDI*	*All*	*Female*	*Main (M)*	*Main (F)*	*Mar (M)*	*Mar (F)*	*LR (M)*	*LR (F)*
Mean	.443	.390	36.880	22.680	42.178	10.475	15.677	53.440	71.258	55.882
Std. Deviation	.2090	.1092	6.024	9.938	1.665	4.417	4.533	6.006	7.04	7.52
CV	47.18	28.0	16.33	43.82	3.94	42.17	28.91	11.24	9.89	13.47
Variance	.043	.011	36.2	98.77	2.774	19.51	20.55	36.07	49.628	56.67
Range	.87	.44	27.27	41.85	6.83	14.83	17.29	24.09	27.71	29.9
Minimum	.01	.21	28.87	8.04	38.27	4.14	10.05	40.32	55.91	42.64
Maximum	.88	.65	56.14	49.89	45.10	18.97	27.34	64.41	83.62	72.54

The sex ratio in Assam has been adverse for many decades. However, during the period 1991-2001 it has improved. As per 2001 census the sex ratio is 932 females per 1000 males, which is marginally below the national average of 933. One of the critical factors which influence their overall development is women's participation in economic activity. The Female Work Participation Rate (FWPR) in the State is less than that of the country as a whole. In Assam 26.59 per cent of total population are main workers as against 30.55 per cent of All India. The percentage of female main workers in the state is 9.68 per cent as against 14.68 per cent in the country as a whole. The male main workers are 42.35 per cent as against 45.35 per cent in the country. In the marginal workers category only 7.58 per cent belong to men and 11.12 per cent as women. Gender disaggregated data on the rural-urban distribution of main workers confirms that most women work in the agricultural sector on family farms and for no wages. Most women workers in the organized sector are employed in the tea gardens. Though tea garden labour is unionized, in practice women have little say in union activities as the unions are male dominated. The high FWPR in the tea industry has not empowered women (AHDR, 2003). There is wide gap in literacy rates between

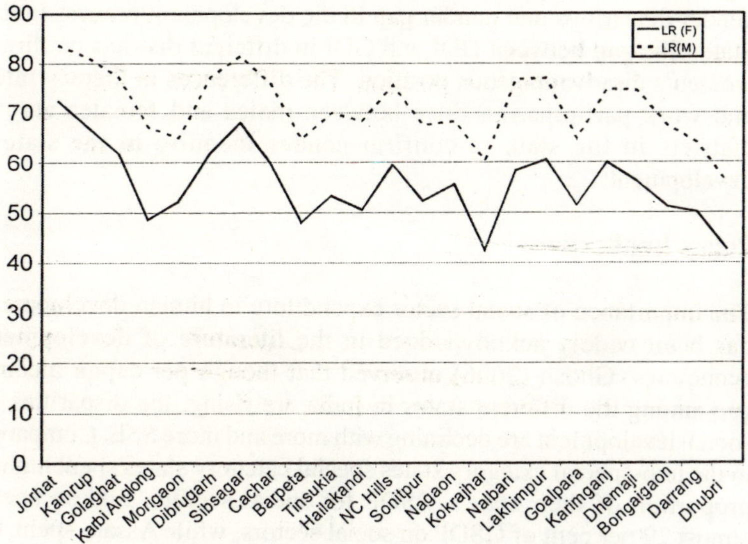

Fig. 6.4: Literacy rates of Males and Females Across Different Districts in Assam

males and females and also wide variation across districts. A large section of SC and ST women are illiterate. Illiteracy among married ST women is 75 per cent, higher than corresponding figure of 45.9 per cent for SC and 56.7 per cent for women in general. Table 6.5 shows some descriptive statistics confirming wide variations of WPR between males and females and also literacy rate. Fig. 6.4 also confirms disparity in literacy rates between males and females.

Conclusions

The present analysis confirms significant variations in the level of achievement in human development in Assam across districts. The bordering districts in lower Assam except Kamrup failed to achieve the performance as that attained by Upper Assam districts. Since the lower Assam districts traditionally experienced higher growth of population due to influx during the days of partition, this might be a causal factor in spatial differences across districts in the state. Among the different components of human development indicators literacy played a vital role in the State, though the health and income indices shows poor performance in determining the value of HDI. The significant and negative value of coefficient of Sex ratio indicates gender disparities and gender gap in the development process in the State. The gap between HDI and GDI in different districts confirms women's disadvantageous position. The differences in literacy rates and work participation rates between males and females across districts in the state re-confirm gender inequity in the state's development.

Policy Implications

The importance of social sector expenditure in human development has been widely acknowledged in the literature of development economics. Ghosh (2006) observed that though per capita income gap among the different states in India are rising; the disparities in social development are declining with more and more SSE. Compared to the non-special category states special category states spent higher proportion of their state's GSDP for social sectors. Sikkim spent almost 29 per cent of GSDP on social sectors, while Assam spent 10 per cent during 2000-05. In most special category states, fiscal priority for social sector registered an increase during the late 1990s, even though it declined thereafter. The per capita SSE expenditure varied from Rs. 5688 for Mizoram to Rs. 1154 for Assam. Analogous to the trend observed among non-special category states, expenditure on education and health together constituted more than half of the total expenditure under SSE in special category states. During the period 2000-01 to 2004-05, expenditure on education for Assam constituted 65 per cent of total expenditure on social services. Expenditure on health however showed a declining trend during the period (RBI, 2006). Thus on the basis of the present analysis the following policy recommendations are suggested:

1. The government should increase social sector expenditure targeting the norm prescribed by the UNDP. In fact considering the low fiscal capacity due to weak financial position the Twelfth Finance Commission has provided specific grants-in-aid to Assam with other six states.
2. The health sector expenditure should receive due priority considering the skewed pattern of health facilities across districts in the State. A specific target oriented programme can only minimize the gap in health facilities in the State.
3. A gender sensitive and participatory development policy must be formulated with a view to address gender disparities in development in the State. Women need to be seen as active partners in the development process.
4. Since a large section of the women among socially disadvantaged group is illiterate and deprived, a targeted approach must be formulated to help this section of population.
5. For empowering women participation in political processes in a meaningful way is important. This should be ensured.
6. The focus of all developmental and poverty alleviation programmes needs to be shifted to women rather than family orientation.

REFERENCES

Assam Human Development Report, 2003: Directorate of Economics and Statistics, Government of Assam.

Dass, S. (1980): *Spotlight on Assam*, Premier Book Service, Chanderpur, Maharashtra.

Dreze, S. and Sen, A.K. (1989), "*Hunger and Public Action*", Oxford University Press, New York.

Fukuda-Parr, Sakiko and A.K. Shiva Kumar (eds.) (2003), *Readings in Human Development*, Second edition, Oxford University Press, New Delhi.

Ghosh, M. (2006), "Economic Growth and Human Development in Indian States", *Economic and Political Weekly*, Vol. 40, No. 30

National Human Development Report, 2001, Planning Commission, New Delhi.

Reserve Bank of India (2007), *State Finances: A Study of Budgets 2006-07*.

Shivakumar, A.K. (1996), "Gender Related development Index: A Comparison for Indian States, *Economic and Political Weekly*, April 16.

7

Human Development among the Workers of Transport Sector in Tripura: A Comparative Study on the Workforce of the Urban Public Modes of Transport

INDRANEEL BHOWMIK

Introduction

The transport sector is unique for the diversity it offers—in the form of (i) vehicles, (ii) pattern of ownership, (iii) purpose of use, and (iv) activity of the worker. Workers of the transport sector are mostly part of the unorganised non-farm sector of the economy that is also called the informal sector in literature. The role played by the transport sector in the development process of an economy is immense and the growth of the transport sector as an integral part of the overall economic growth is unquestionable. Another important concomitant to development is urbanisation. Growth of urban centres results in the expansion of the urban transport system. Apart from the private transport machineries the demand and use of the public modes also increase. City buses, metro rails, cabs, trams, etc. are the most common form of public conveyance. Moreover, in small Indian cities we also find local innovations.

The urban public transport in Tripura can be broadly classified into four categories—(i) auto (three-wheelers); (ii) jeeps; (iii) taxis/vans; and (iv) rickshaws. Interestingly, rickshaw-pullers are not recognised within the transport system (NCEUS, 2008) yet one can never ignore this vital component of the urban public transport in the state. Town or city buses used to run earlier but had been withdrawn by the government in the early 1990s. Three-wheelers generally run on specific routes along the main roads within the urban limits, jeeps also ply on specific routes but for a bit longer routes connecting one place to other. There are no metered taxis in Tripura but cars and vans can be hired for specific purposes at pre-determined rates and these operate in the state like cabs with the passenger determining the routes. Apart from these automated vehicles we find human operated rickshaws available. The rickshaws do not have any specific route and the passenger is free to determine its pathway. Generally, rickshaws play on small distances and have no qualms in moving to the branch roads. It should be noted here that the first three categories of vehicles need permit from the state transport department to operate while the last mode requires licence from the urban municipal bodies. Moreover, the first three requires a valid driving licence for the driver while there are no such bindings on the rickshaw puller. It is thus obvious that driving is a specialised job while turning out to be rickshaw puller calls for no special skill, therefore, it is likely that there will be sizeable variation among the workers of the different modes of transport.

Objective of the Study

The present paper stems in order to assess the human development levels of the workers of the transport sector. The specific objectives of the paper are—

1. To analyse the socio-demographic condition of the workers of the urban passenger modes of transport, i.e., short distance travels.
2. To find out the levels of human development of the workers engaged in the urban public transport system.
3. To compute the Human Development Measure (HDM) and compare the levels of Human Development among the workers of various categories.

Methodology

In order to address the above objectives, both primary and secondary data have been used. Various government offices, trade union offices and institutions have been the source for secondary data. Primary data have been collected through a sample survey of the targeted group in Agartala on the basis of a pre-structured schedule. It should be noted here that the distribution of vehicles in Tripura are highly skewed in favour of the West districts and more particularly Agartala city as 80 per cent of the vehicles are from that region.

A composite index, Human Development Measure (HDM) has been constructed comprising the three major indicators of human development—education, health and income. Each attribute has been measured in terms of an index, which is relative to the performance of the best in the category; and all the independent index have been compiled to form the final human development measure. In order to understand the levels of education among the sample the framework of 'Likert' scale has been used. The health criterion is analysed using information regarding the incidence of disease in the immediate past one-year period (September 2006—August 2007). A total of 76 diseases/ailments were identified and inquired from the respondents. These 76 diseases have been further classified in 20 ailment groups (Table 7.1) for easier comprehension. The earning of the respondents during the previous month (August 2007) is considered as the indicator of income. In other words, we say,

- Scores for the three major parameters are obtained using the best performer (category) among the sub-sectors as a benchmark.
- For Income the maximum average income per month is considered to be the benchmark and the Income Measure (YM) is calculated.
- For Education the maximum score as per Liker scaling is the benchmark and it provides the basis for the Educational Measure (EM).
- For Health, the least affected by disease, i.e., the lowest per capita disease is regarded to be the benchmark which helps in determining the Good Health Measure (GHM).
- The HDM is calculated on the lines of the Human Development Index (HDI) and is basically the average of the three independent measures.

Thus, HDM = (GHM+ EM+YM)/3 and the scores lie between 0 and 1

Sample Profile

Table 7.1: Number of public means of transport operating in Agartala city

Category	*Population*	*Representative Sample*
Auto (Three-wheelers)	2559	90
Jeeps	940	35
Taxis/Vans/Cars	286	12
Rickshaws	2347	83
Total	6132	220

Source: Computed from data collected from all the respective trade union offices.

The respondents were selected using stratified random sampling. Representative samples were drawn from each stratum following a proportion of 3.5 per cent of the total population. Moreover, assistants and cleaners have been ignored for the present study as they are mostly apprentice and do not have any independent existence as worker. Table 7.1 attests to the sample structure. In all, the study is made on the basis of the responses provided by 220 workers of the urban passenger transport system who were selected randomly in the final stage and the survey was conducted in the month of August 2007 at Agartala city.

Age and Family Size

Table 7.2: Age and Family size of the respondents

Category	*Age*			*Family Size*		
	Average	*Max*	*Min*	*Average*	*Max*	*Min*
Auto (Three-wheelers)	31.89	55	14	4.61	8	1
Jeeps	28.5	47	18	4.21	8	3
Taxis/Vans/Cars	28	37	19	5.08	9	3
Rickshaws	36.8	60	16	4.47	7	1

Source: Primary Survey.

Table 7.2 shows that the rickshaw pullers of Agartala are comparatively older than the workers of other vehicles even though the youngest member of the sample is an auto driver. Interestingly, this youngest respondent was in the third month of his working life as an auto driver and had no valid licence. However, there is not much difference in the family size of the workers of different categories.

Access to Basic Amenities

Table 7.3: Availability of Sanitation, drinking water, electricity facilities among respondents

(*In percentage*)

Category	Sanitation			Drinking Water[1]		Electricity	
	Perma-nent	Tempo-rary	None[2]	Pure	Impure	No	Yes
Auto (Three-wheelers)	48.88	51.12	0.00	45.55	54.45	5.41	94.44
Jeeps	57.14	40.00	2.86	37.14	62.86	20.00	80.00
Taxis/Vans/Cars	66.67	25.00	8.33	58.33	41.67	8.33	91.67
Rickshaws	38.55	50.60	11.85	36.14	63.86	22.89	77.11

Notes: 1. Pure refers to potable water supplied by Agartala Municipal Council and filtered thereafter, while impure is for any other form.
2. None refers to absence of any latrine in the house or place of dwelling.

Source: Primary Survey.

The basic amenities enjoyed by the workers cannot be considered satisfactory. Table 7.3 shows that only 66.67 per cent of the car drivers enjoy permanent sanitary facility in their residences while this facility is least for the rickshaw pullers, being as low as 38.55 per cent. In regards to the quality of drinking water, we find these two categories—cars and rickshaws to be to at the two ends of the spectrum with 58.33 per cent and 36.14 per cent using pure water respectively. However, for the electricity facility, the auto drivers are a shade better than the car drivers with only 5.56 per cent of them bereft with power connection at their homes, while the rickshaw pullers stand at the nadir.

Housing Pattern

Mud walls are the most prominent form among the houses of all categories of respondents. Incidence of brick walls is comparatively higher among car drivers while bamboo made houses is used by almost

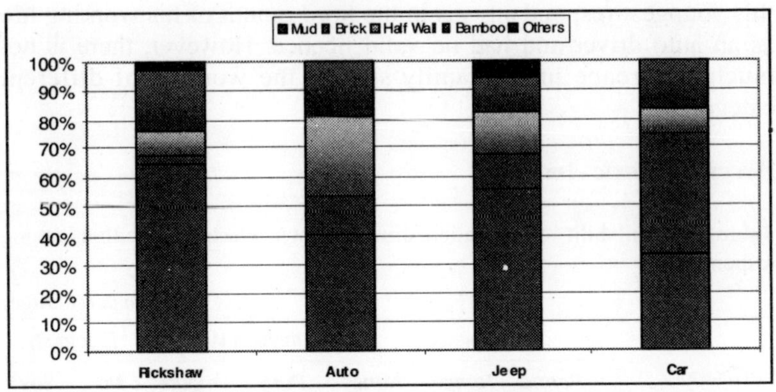

Fig 7.1: Type of walls used by the respondents

15 per cent of the respondents across different categories. More than 27 per cent of the auto drivers live in half-walled houses. On the other hand tin is the most popular form of roof material among all groups. Concrete roof is found only for two Auto drivers and one car driver. The traditional form of roof in Tripura, i.e. thatch is declining, as its incidence is much lower amidst all categories of respondents.

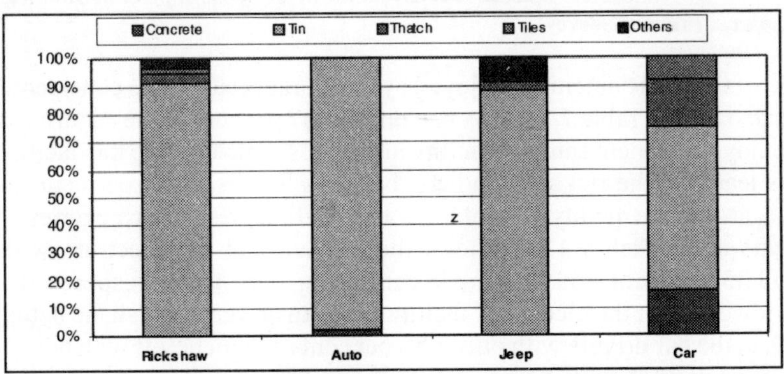

Fig 7.2: Type of roof used by the respondents

Access to Public Distribution System Facility

Table 7.4 shows that majority of the auto, jeep and car drivers belong to the above poverty line, while most of the rickshaw pullers are from the BPL category. Interestingly, there are 12 rickshaw pullers who do not have any ration card. They are in most cases illegal migrants from Bangladesh and a few claim to be victims of political rivalry.

Table 7.4: Nature of ration card holdings among the respondents

(in percentage)

	Above Poverty Line	*Below Poverty Line*	*Antyodaya*	*None*
Auto (Three-wheelers)	81.11	18.89	0.00	0.00
Jeeps	65.71	28.50	0.00	5.71
Taxis/Vans/Cars	91.67	8.33	0.00	0.00
Rickshaws	34.94	48.19	2.41	14.45

Source: Primary Survey.

Financial Status

Table 7.5: Status of finance among the respondents

(in percentage)

	Bank Account[1]	*Insurance*[2]	*Loan*[3]	*Savings*
Auto (Three-wheelers)	55.55	44.44	32.22	55.55
Jeeps	51.43	37.14	2.85	60.00
Taxis/Vans/Cars	66.66	33.33	0	75.00
Rickshaws	6.02	21.11	9.64	40.96

Notes: 1. Operational on the date of interview;
2. Premium paid within the previous year;
3. Loan repayment in the process and includes personal and business loans.

Source: Primary Survey.

The most encouraging fact regarding the financial status of the respondents is that a sizeable section of them have made some savings. 44.44 per cent of the auto drivers pay life-insurance premiums and even 21.11 per cent of the rickshaw pullers do it. Some of the auto drivers and rickshaw pullers have availed bank or institutional finance for their vehicle under different development and self-employment generation programmes of the government and thus maintains a bank account.

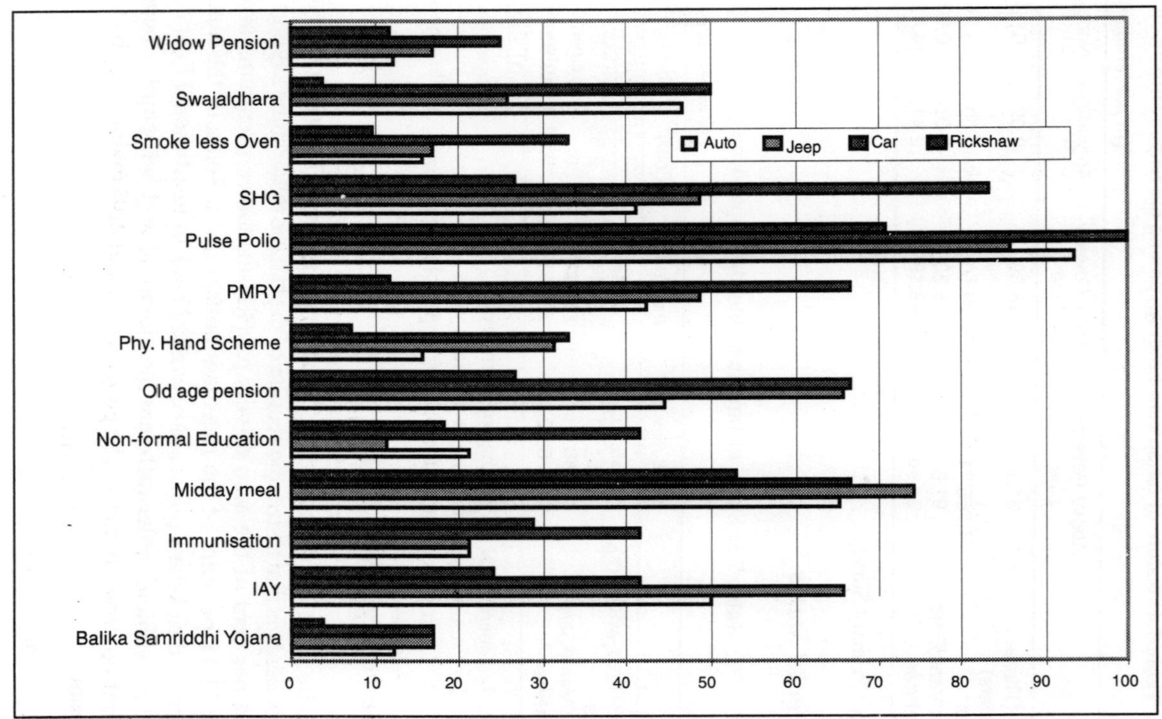

Fig 7.3: Awareness of government programmes

Awareness

Pulse polio is the most popular government programme among all the categories of transport workers as is evident in Fig 7.3. On the other hand, the respondents were least aware about the Balika Samriddhi Yojana. Among the other programmes, the concept of Self-Help Groups (SHGs). Mid-day meal, Old age pension is also quite well known. The Pradhan Mantri Rozgar Yojana is well known to the auto drivers. The Jeep drivers are better aware about the Indira Awaas Yojana. Interestingly, the auto drivers exhibit higher wakefulness for most of the programmes as compared to the other categories except for Non-formal education and Mid-day meal. In contrast, the rickshaw-pullers depict the least awareness for all the schemes excluding Non-formal education and immunisation programme.

Education

Education is one of the most significant attribute and basically an asset to the individual. The average number of years of schooling of non-agricultural workers of India is 6.5 years (NCEUS, 2008) that is indicative of the completion of the primary level. However, the level of education among the respondents as shown in Table 7.6, suggest wide variation among the different categories of the transport workers. Majority of the rickshaw pullers are illiterate even though there are no illiterates in other categories. Only one auto-driver is a graduate and another has completed the Higher Secondary level. Most of the respondents have completed the senior basic level and have mostly

Table 7.6: Levels of Education among the respondents

(In percentage)

	Illiterate	*Primary*	*Class VIII*	*Class X*	*H.S & Above*	*Total*
Auto (Three-wheelers)	0	27 (30)	49 (54.44)	12 (13.33)	2 (2.22)	90
Jeeps	0	7 (20)	26 (74.29)	2 (5.71)	0	35
Taxis/Vans/ Cars	0	1 (8.33)	9 (75)	2 (16.67)	0	12
Rickshaws	44 (53.01)	19 (28.92)	15 (18.07)	0	0	83
Total	44	54	99	14	2	220

Note: Figures in brackets indicate per cent.

Source: Primary Survey.

dropped out of education owing to failure in clearing the Madhyamik or matriculation examination. The educational status of the rickshaw pullers is worse and as expected there are no matriculates, even though a few of them did appear at the examination but failed to clear it.

Health

Table 7.7 shows that 291 cases of disease and ailment have been identified among 220 respondents. Rickshaw-pullers are most prone to ailments, as 179 cases have been reported while the total incidence is least for car drivers though per capita incidence of disease is lowest for jeep drivers. The most common ailment among the respondents was linked to cold and cough followed by gastro related

Table 7.7: Incidence of disease among the respondents

	Auto (Three-wheelers)	*Jeeps*	*Taxis/ Vans/ Cars*	*Rickshaws*	*Total*
Asthma	2 (2.22)	0	0	10 (12.05)	12
Bone (tumour & disorders)	5 (5.56)	1 (2.86)	0.00	5 (6.02)	11
Chest and Heart	7 (7.78)	0	1 (8.33)	37 (44.58)	45
Cold/Cough/Fever/Sinus	17(18.89)	7 (20.00)	5 (41.67)	20 (24.10)	49
Diabetes	5 (5.56)	0	0	0	5
Ear disorder	3 (3.33)	0	0	5 (6.02)	8
Eye disorder	5 (5.56)	0	1 (8.33)	5 (6.02)	11
Gastro related disorders	3 (3.33)	8 (22.86)	4 (33.33)	22 (26.51)	37
Headache	10 (11.11)	0	3 (25)	10 (12.05)	23
High BP/hypertension	0	0	1 (8.33)	5 (6.02)	6
Jaundice	0	0	0	2 (2.41)	2
Low BP	5 (5.56)	2 (5.71)	0	9 (10.84)	16
Malaria	0	0	0	3 (3.61)	3
Piles	2 (2.22)	0	0	4 (4.82)	6
Skin disorders (including allergy)	0	0	0	15 (18.07)	15
Sore Throat	0	0	1 (8.33)	3 (3.61)	4
Spondilysis	3 (3.33)	1 (2.86)	0	5 (6.02)	9
Toothache	8 (8.89)	1 (2.86)	0	9 (10.84)	18
Tuberculosis	0	1 (2.86)	0	5 (6.02)	6
Urological Problems	0	0	0	5 (6.02)	5
Aggregate	75	21	16	179	291
Per capita disease	0.83	0.60	1.25	2.16	1.32

Source: Primary Survey.
Note: Figures in brackets indicate per cent.

disorders; both of which occur due to irregular life-style and food habit. Another grave concern is the high incidence of chest and heart related problems for rickshaw pullers; almost 45 per cent of the respondents face such agony owing to the hard physical strain and labour they put in. It should be here noted that the higher average age of the rickshaw puller is also responsible for higher incidence of disease. Interesting to note here that incidence of life-style disease like diabetes and hypertension is less prevalent among the workers of the transport sector.

Income

The data on monthly income suggest that most of the respondents, as high as 112, fall in the earning bracket of Rs. 2001–Rs. 3000 and this income class has the highest frequency for auto drivers, jeep drivers and rickshaw pullers independently also. On the other hand, as many as six rickshaw-pullers and one jeep driver has reported a monthly

Table 7.8: Monthly incomes of the respondents

	Auto	*Jeep*	*Car*	*Rickshaw*	*Total*
≤1000	0	1 (2.86)	0	6 (7.23)	7
1001-2000	8 (8.89)	5 (14.28)	4 (33.33)	19 (22.89)	36
2001-3000	47 (52.22)	18 (51.43)	3 (25)	44 (53.01)	112
3001-4000	24 (26.67)	5 (14.28)	2 (16.67)	10 (12.05)	41
4001-5000	6 (6.67)	3 (8.57)	1 (8.33)	4 (4.82)	14
5001≤	5 (5.55)	3 (8.57)	2 (16.67)	0	10
Total	90	35	12	83	**220**
Average	3364.71	3265.74	3291.67	2555.42	—
Std. Dev	1636.34	1076.75	1590.00	950.74	—
Max	7500	10000	6000	4500	10000
Min	2000	1000	1500	700	700
Range	5500	9000	4500	3800	9300

Note: Figures in brackets indicate per cent.

Source: Primary Survey.

income of less than Rs. 1000, while the highest monthly income earned among the respondents of Rs. 10000, is also by a jeep driver. In all only 10 respondents affirmed income above Rs. 5000 per month, five of them were auto-drivers and none of the rickshaw pullers came into that income class. The average monthly income is highest for the auto-drivers while it is expectedly least for the rickshaw pullers. However, the standard deviation is least for the rickshaw pullers and highest for the auto-drivers. The maximum range of income is for the jeep drivers whereas the least is for the rickshaw pullers.

In order to identify the level of variation in income among different groups the adjoining regression was carried out

$$Y = a + b_1D_1 + b_2D_2 + b_3D_3 + \mu$$

where a, b_1, b_2 and b_3 are the regression coefficients; a = income of the auto-drivers

D_1 = Dummy value '1' for Jeep drivers, '0' for others;
D_2 = Dummy value '1' for car drivers, '0' for others; and
D_3 = Dummy value '1' for rickshaw pullers, '0' for others.

Table 7.9: Regression Results

	B	*Std. Error*	*t*	*Sig.*
Auto (a)	3364.444	123.427	27.259	0.000
Jeep (D1)	-98.730	233.255	-0.423	0.673
Car (D2)	-72.778	359.849	-0.202	0.840
Rickshaw (D3)	-809.023	178.195	-4.54	0.000

F= 7.660***

The regression results indicate highly significant variation in the income of the rickshaw pullers with that of the others. However, the differences in the income among the other three categories are not significant.

The Human Development Aspect

The Human Development Measure (HDM) is prepared through the combination of the Education Measure (EM); the Good Health Measure (GHM) and the Income Measure (YM).

Educational Measure (EM) is calculated on the basis of the educational score, which indicates the representative level of education. The final EM is derived in two stages.

Stage 1

Using the principle of "Likert Scaling" we rate the different level of education in the following way:

1. = illiterate
2. = primary level
3. = Class VIII level
4. = Class X or Matriculation
5. = Class XII and Higher

Educational Score (ES_i) for the ith group = Σ [{proportional distribution of the ith group in the class} × {rating}],

Table 7.10: Educational Score

	Educational Score*
Auto (Three-wheelers)	287.74
Jeeps	285.71
Taxis/Vans/Cars	308.34
Rickshaws	165.06

Source: Computed.

Stage 2

Having computed the Educational Score for each stratum we calculate the Educational Measure:

$$EM_i = ES_i/\text{Max ES}$$

Good Health Measure (GHM) is calculated on the basis of the per capita disease. It is presumed that good health indicates less incidence of disease, i.e. per capita disease will be less. Thus,

$$GHM_i = \text{MIN [Per capita disease]/[Per capita disease]}_i$$

Income Measure (YM) is more easily calculated on the basis of the average monthly income (AMY); Thus,

$$YM_i = (AMY)_i/MAX\ (AMY)$$

Table 7.11: Human Development Measure (HDM), Educational Measure (EM), Good Health Measure (GHM) and Income Measure (YM) of the respondents

	EM	*GHM*	*YM*	*HDM*
Auto (Three-wheelers)	0.933191	0.722892	1	0.885361
Jeeps	0.926607	1	0.970655	0.965754
Taxis/Vans/Cars	1	0.48	0.978369	0.819456
Rickshaws	0.535318	0.277778	0.759538	0.524211

Thus, Table 7.11 shows that as expected, the rickshaw pullers are at the bottom of the human development indicators among the various segments of transport workers. The jeep drivers emerge as the front-runner in the development process on the basis of human development indicators. However, the most interesting feature is that the three categories of automotive vehicle drivers considered in the present study each emerge as the best performer in one section. However, in terms of the health measure, the jeep drivers appear to be in much better condition than others which ultimately determines their rank in terms of Human Development Measure.

Conclusion

The workforce engaged in the transport sector are part of the huge unorganised sector of the Indian economy, as a result, they share the multitude of problems that exist in their work place and ambience. Yet the most important conclusion from the study is that there are wide scale differentials in the socio-economic condition and the human development levels of the various segments of the transport workers with the rickshaw-pullers lying at the rock bottom. It is obvious that rickshaw-pullers possess lesser skills and the nature of the job confine them to lesser income levels but the most worrisome factor is the huge gap between them and the others regarding the education and health attributes. Often it is seen that lower educational skill is a factor for becoming a rickshaw-puller and it also acts as a barrier for graduation to other forms of automotive vehicles. Naturally it will be a welcome step if the policy-makers take step to minimise the differentials through emphasis on these two aspects—education and health. Special attention may be provided for non-formal education and health camps or preventive medical facilities for the practising rickshaw pullers, which will boost up their livelihood micro context and foster the state economy with healthy and educated workforce in the macro context.

REFERENCES

Government of Tripura (2006): *Basic Statistics of Tripura.*

Government of Tripura (2007): *Economic Review of Tripura.*

Government of Tripura (2007): *Tripura Human Development Report.*

Government of Tripura (undated), *Tripura State Development Report* (Draft).

Gujrati, D.N., (2004) *Essentials of Econometrics*, Tata McGraw-Hill Edition (4th Reprint), New Delhi.

Kartikeyan, S., Gurav R.B., Joshi S.D., Wayal Reshma (2004); Health and Socio-demographic profile of Transport Workers; *Indian Journal of Occupational and Environmental Medicine*, Vol. 8, No. 2.

NCEUS, Government of India (2008), Report on Conditions of Work and Promotion of Livelihoods in the Unorganised Sector.

Tripura Darpan (2007) Tathyapanji-O-Nirdeshika.

UNDP (2007); *Human Development Primer.*

8

Migration and Development: Implications for Human Development

TARUN BIKASH SUKAI

Since the very beginning of the humanity, people have migrated. Migratory flows have always been an integral part as well as a major determinant of human history. Over the last two centuries, migration rose to an unprecedented level, primarily owing to the globalization of economic activity and its effect on labour migration. While majority of them are internal migrants, the number of international migrants is also quite substantial. International migrants now constitute the world's fifth most populous country if they all lived in the same place—after China, India, U.S.A. and Indonesia. The number of people living outside their country of birth has almost doubled during the last 50 years—increasing to 191 million in 2005 (UN, 2006a). Women now constitute almost half of all migrants and dominate in migration streams to developed countries. The proportion of international migrants worldwide has grown from 2.5 per cent of the total global population in1960 to 2.9 per cent in 2000. The number of new international migrants was 36 million between 1990 and 2005. Out of this, 33 million migrated to industrialized countries. These trends reveal that 75 per cent of all international migrants now live in 28 countries (UN, 2006b). The net migration accounts for a growing and major share of population growth in developed regions—three quarters in 2000-2005.

Causes of Migration

International migration is a vital part of today's globalize existence. It can play a key role in development and poverty reduction. The benefits of migration could be enhanced and its disadvantages can be minimized. International migration has tended to be seen primarily in development terms, as a response to disparities in income levels and unequal employment opportunities between countries. Poverty and unemployment are often indicated as the main 'push factors', which impels individuals to leave their home countries, and cross-border differences in wage levels and employment opportunities are among the 'pull factors'. Migration can be forced or voluntary. Growing interdependence between countries and widening inequalities will probably lead to the further intensification of international movements. If their economies continue to grow, developed countries will require more migrants to undertake low-paying work that their native counterparts are unable or unwilling to do. These jobs known as 4Ds: dirty, difficult, demeaning and dangerous includes garbage collection, street cleaning, construction, mining, sex work, etc. (GCIM, 2005). On the other hand, the demand for highly skilled professionals in technological, managerial, scientific or administrative activities is also increasing. Most rich countries are open to and indeed encourage immigration at the top end of skill range, but are ambiguous or negative about their need at the lower range. The global competition is driving countries to recruit more highly skilled migrant workers in order to maintain and increase their economic edge. As a result, researchers estimate that between a third and half of the developing world's science and technology personnel now live in the developed world (Lowell *et al.*, 2004). Recent WHO surveys show that the intention to migrate is especially high among the health workers living in the regions, hit hardest with HIV/AIDS—68 per cent in Zimbabwe and 26 per cent in Uganda (Awases *et al.*, 2004). Each year between 30 per cent and 50 per cent South African health graduates leave their countries for U.K. and U.S.A. Researchers observe that small and less developed countries are most likely to suffer from the effects of brain-drain (Thouez 2005). For example, in 2000 over 70 per cent of the highly educated population of Guyana, Haiti, Jamaica, and Trinidad and Tobago were living in OECD countries (UN, 2006b). Many countries are increasingly reluctant to receive large number of permanent migrants, but widening social and economic disparities could lead to great number of undocumented migrants willing to flout regulations in exchange for the promise of a better life. Undocumented migrants confront huge risks while attempting to reach their destination. Every year newspapers are filled with stories of those who did not make it—migrants who drowned or died of exposure or murdered by unscrupulous smugglers.

Forced migration and trafficking, on the other hand, encompass the more poignant vulnerabilities associated with international movements—particularly where it involves women and children. The best-known group with the forced migration is that of "refugees", people who flee their own countries hit by war, violence and chaos, and who are unable or unwilling to return to home countries because they lack effective protection. In 2005, there were 12.7 million refugees and they constitute 7 per cent of all migrants (UNHCR, 2006a). Unlike labour migrants, who tend to move towards developed regions, an estimated 90 per cent of all refugees currently live in developing countries (UNHCR, 2006b). Most refugees seek safe havens in countries bordering their own. Asylum seekers are individuals who apply for recognition of their refugee status in another country or at embassy, and who usually must wait pending a decision from an appropriate body. Asylum-seekers whose applications are rejected often can't be deported because the country of origin will not take them back, or they lack passports. They often end up labouring in more insecure and unregulated informal economy as laws frequently bar them from seeking jobs in the formal sector. There has been relatively little research from a human rights perspective into the reasons why migrants move. There is a need to go beyond economic explanations of migration, which focus on income poverty. We also need to focus on human poverty, which also takes into account—e.g. Lack of health care, food and education, and inequality of opportunity including gender discrimination (HDR, 2000). Thus, the deficits in human rights and development can be the major cause of migration.

Contribution of Migrant Workers

The Global Commission on International Migration (GCIM) identified two broad types of contributions of migrants. Firstly, they are contributing to the growth, development and poverty reduction in the countries of their origin. Secondly, to the countries of destination by filling the gaps in labour market, by providing essential skills, and by bringing social, cultural and intellectual dynamism to the societies that migrants have joined (GCIM, 2005).

The impact of 'brain drain' is more ambiguous. Though it takes the advantages of skill away from the countries of origin, it also means that highly skilled migrants can earn higher incomes and they also gain added skills that enable them to contribute more to their home countries. In monetary terms, remittances rang in at about US$ 232 billion—out of which developing countries received $167 billion as estimated by the World Bank in 2005 (World Bank, 2006). The actual amount of remittances may be higher, since this figure does not take into account funds transferred through non-formal channels. The remittance is considered as the second-largest source of external funding for developing countries after the Foreign Direct Investment (FDI). Some of the most visible forms of contributions of migrants to the countries of origin are the remittance of private funds and material goods, by individual migrants to their families; the support given by the diaspora organizations to their home towns, and the return of migrants who have gained qualifications abroad. Though measuring the impact of remittances in terms of poverty reduction is difficult, there appears to be a positive link between remittances and strengthening human rights. At the household level, remittances help in improving children's education, and in contributing to better health, housing and family welfare. Similarly when migrants' associations raise and transmit fund to build schools or community health centres, this increases the availability and accessibility of education and health. Again teachers, doctors or lawyers in diaspora communities are assisted through similar projects to contribute the skills they have gained abroad to their home countries. Every Millennium Development Goal (MDG) has some direct or indirect linkage with migration. Remittances play an important role to eradicate extreme poverty and hunger (MDG-1), to provide universal elementary education (MDG-2) and to improve health (MDG-4, 5, 6). Migration also contributes to promote gender equality and empower women (MDG-3). Migration can also have a positive impact on the society of origin through other effects. In general, migration may lead to an enriching exchange with other cultures.

Migration also brings a wide range of gains to countries of destination. It includes the greater social benefits, better welfare and increased social services for citizens—which flow from migration and are the result of a larger tax base and greater social security funds, higher level of entrepreneurship and a younger population in demographic terms. It is estimated that migrants in the UK contributed

£31.2 billion in taxes, and increased public expenditure by £28.8 billion through their receipt of public goods and services, resulting in a net fiscal contribution of around £2.5 billion[1]. Women migrants also contribute to development by allowing women in countries of destination to lead professional lives by taking their place as caregivers for children and the elderly. Until few years ago, there was virtual absence of gender in policy intervention on migration. But today it is evident that a specific demand for female labour exists, generated by global growth of service sector requiring personalized services, including but not limited to domestic work, care of old and sick.

The World Bank observed that there is a considerable support for the view that migrants create new business, jobs, fill labour market gaps, improving productivity and reducing inflationary pressures (World Bank, 2006).

Violation of Migrants' Human Rights

Despite this, many of the issues surrounding migration are complex and sensitive. The introduction of people from one culture to another tends to generate suspicion. Fear and down right xenophobia. The degree of vulnerability differs between two extremes. At one end of the migration spectrum are the highly skilled, who voluntarily leave their home country to take employment in another country, to which they travel and which they enter legally, and in which they have regular immigration status. At the other end of spectrum are the men, women and children whose decision to move is made at the instigation of a trafficker or who engage the services of smuggler; who enter the country of destination illegally through dangerous routes; whose immigration status is irregular and who are likely to work in conditions of exploitation. Among the rights that all migrants should enjoy, one can notably mention the following: freedom of thought, conscience and religion; protection of their security and liberty; access to investigations, arrests and detentions carried out in accordance with established procedures; joining or forming trade unions and associations; equality with nationals in gaining access to education; transfer of their earnings; information in a language they understand about their rights; treatment as equal to nationals regarding remuneration and conditions of work, social security benefits and emergency medical care (ICMW, 2003). For a larger portion of migrants, working conditions are abusive and exploitative and may be characterized by forced labour, low wages, poor working environment, a virtual absence of social protection, the denial of freedom of association and trade union rights, discrimination and xenophobia as well as social exclusion—all of which rob workers of the benefits of working in another country (ILO, 2004).

At times of political tension, they may be the first to be suspected or scape-goated as security risks; by linking anti-terrorism and immigration control in the context of the 'war on terror', many governments have encouraged unintentionally xenophobia against migrants from particular regions of the world. Because of their condition both as migrants and as women, the women migrants are 'double marginalised' and are particularly vulnerable to exploitation and ill treatment. From its review of country situations, the CERD Committee has noted the serious problems commonly faced by migrant domestic workers such as debt bondage, passport retention, illegal confinement, rape and physical assault.[2]

Inadequate data on international migration is a general problem and it is acute in case of human rights. Violations have been generally under-recorded. The irregular migrants may be reluctant to seek protection against rights abuse from the police or employment authorities because they fear deportation. Migrants' lack of familiarity with the laws and procedures of their host countries can also contribute to under-reporting of abuse and consequent lack of data. In some countries, national employment laws do not protect migrant workers, in fact they are likely to work in informal sector of employment where labour standards are not applied. Even destination countries with sophisticated data collection capacities do not know the scale of trafficking flows. Because conventional methods of data collection can't easily be adapted to different situations involving trafficking, smuggling and other illegal forms of activities.

Mechanisms for Protecting Migrants' Rights

There is a growing body of reporting on migrants' rights within the UN human rights system. This has been developed through the work of the Human Rights Commission's special procedures. All persons, regardless of their nationality, race, legal or other status, are entitled to fundamental human rights and basic labour protections including migrant workers and their families. Migrants are also entitled to certain human rights and protections specifically linked to their vulnerable status. Governments' obligations to ensuring the human rights of migrant workers includes the excerpts from the Migration for Employment Convention No.97 (revised), the Migrant Workers (Supplementary Provisions) Convention No.143, Universal Declaration of Human Rights, the International Covenant on Economic,. Social and Cultural Rights (ICESCR), the International Covenant on Civil and Political Rights (ICCPR), the Convention on the Elimination of All Forms of Discrimination Against Women (CEDAW), the Convention on the Elimination of All Forms of Racial Discrimination (CERD), the Convention on the Rights of the Child (CRC), ILO Labour Convention (No.29), the ILO Freedom of Association and Protection of the Right to Organise Convention (No.87), the ILO Equal Remuneration Convention (No.100), the ILO Discrimination (Employment and Occupation) Convention (No.111), the ILO Minimum Age Convention (No.38), and the International Convention on the Protection of the Rights of All Migrant Workers and Members of Their Families (ICMW). Governments' commitments to ensuring human rights of migrant workers also include commitment made at the World Conference on Human Rights in Vienna, the International Conference on Population and Development in Cairo, the World Summit for Social Development in Copenhagen and the World Conference on Women in Beijing.

The ICMW applies to all the universal human rights by taking into account the particular situation of migrant workers and their family members. It also provides the first international definition of migrant workers and of certain specific categories (such as frontier workers, seasonal workers, itinerant workers or self-employed workers). It is worth noting, however, that the Convention seeks to establish basic principles of their treatment and to establish norms, which will contribute to the harmonization of states' attitudes towards migration through acceptance of these basic principles. It also requires actions by states to prevent and eliminate clandestine movements and trafficking and to eliminate the employment of irregular migrants by employers. It also says that 'entering a country in violation of its immigration laws does not deprive migrants of the fundamental human rights nor does it affect the obligation of states to protect migrants in an irregular situation' (GCIM, 2005). States' duties under international law are not limited to respecting, protecting and fulfilling human rights through the acts of state institutions and officials, but also to protect individuals against violation by private persons. This is of great importance to migrants since many migrants work in the informal economy and in domestic work. If migrants are to enjoy these protections, international laws must be implemented by states.

But unfortunately, most of the developed countries did not ratify ICMW (See Table 8.1). After adoption by the UN General Assembly in 1990, the Convention was open to ratification by states. Ratifications of Convention by at least 20 member states were

Table 8.1: Status of Ratification of international legal instruments related to international migration

Parties to UN Instruments			
Instruments Percentage of Countries	*Year entered into force*	*No. of Countries*	*Parties to UN*
Migrant Workers			
• 1949 ILO Convention Migration for employment (Revised) (No.97)	1952	45	23
• 1979 ILO Convention concerning migration in Abusive Conditions and Promotion of Equality of Opportunity and Treatment of Migrant Workers (Supplementary Provision) (No.143)	1978	19	10
• 1990 International Convention on the Protection of the Rights of all Migrant Workers and Members of their Families	2003	34	17
Smuggling and Trafficking			
• 2000 Protocol to Prevent, Suppress and Punish Trafficking in Persons especially Women and Children	2003	97	50
• 2000 Protocol against the Smuggling of Migrants by Land, Sea and Air	2004	89	46
Refugees			
• 1951 Convention relating the status of Refugees	1954	143	73
• 1967 Protocol relating the status of Refugees	1967	143	73

Source: United Nations, 2006. *International Migration and Development: Report of the Secretary-General* (A/60/871).

necessary in order for the Convention to enter into force. It took 13 years to reach this threshold in 2003 and presently the Convention has been ratified by 34 states (2006). All these states are on the sending side of the migration process. Being concerned by the situation of their citizens living abroad, they view the Convention as part of a strategy to protect their emigrants. Important sending countries such as Mexico, Morocco and the Philippines have thus ratified the Convention. The ratification record of the Convention on Migrants' Rights is extremely low in comparison to other UN treaties. The impact of the Convention is further diminished by the fact that no major receiving state—including Europe, North America and Australia—has ratified the Convention. The countries that have done so are having only a very small percentage of the world's total migrant population, implying that most migrants are currently not protected by this Convention.

Hardly any research has been conducted on the reasons behind states' reluctance to ratify the Convention. A major difficulty is that only very few states have actually provided an explanation on the reasons why they did not consider ratification. Most states have been largely indifferent and this absence of official reaction makes it difficult to identify the obstacles. In order to have more detailed information on the obstacles to the Convention, UNESCO commissioned reports in several regions of the world. On this basis, four kinds of obstacles have been identified. A first set of problems stems from the content of the Convention, or from what is wrongly understood as being the content of the Convention. Secondly, states may experience administrative difficulties in ratifying and implementing the Convention. Thirdly, they may see ratification as leading to costs, which they cannot afford. Fourthly, wide ranges of political considerations hinder the ratification of the Convention.[3]

This striking lack of interest is also partly due to the fact that the Convention on Migrants' Rights is a relatively marginal one: it does not belong to the six core UN Conventions[4] and has never been given much priority. Until 1996, it was even difficult to have access to the text of the Convention and that no single person anywhere in the world was working full-time on issues surrounding it (TARAN, 2000a). A general source of difficulties regarding the ratification of the UN Convention is social transformations, which took place in the world during the last three decades. The Convention was thought of in the seventies, drafted in the eighties and opened to ratification in the nineties. During this time period, international migration and the world in general—went through massive changes which partly explains why the Convention appeared less relevant than initially expected. It was drafted on the basis of states' experience with migration in the seventies and its application to more recent migration challenges is therefore not absolutely straightforward (Lonnroth, 1991).

Migration, Development and Human Rights

Development can be defined in both senses: as economic development which leads to economic growth; and as human development which focuses on the individual, his family and community and seeks to expand individual capabilities and choices through health, education, a decent standard of living and political freedom.

1. The International Covenant on Economic, Social and Cultural Rights (ICESCR, adopted in 1966 and entered into force in 1976),
2. The International Covenant on Civil and Political Rights (ICCPR, 1966-1976),
3. The International Convention on the Elimination of All Forms of Racial Discrimination (CERD, 1965-1969),
4. The Convention on the Elimination of All Forms of Discrimination Against Women (CEDAW, 1979-1980),
5. The Convention Against Torture and Other Cruel, Inhuman or Degrading Treatment or Punishment (CAT, 1984-1987),
6. The Convention on the Rights of the Child (CRC, 1989-1990).

Development must entail fuller realization of economic, social and cultural rights on the one hand and civil and political rights on the other. By postulating the pursuit of one set of rights to the neglect of others do not constitute development. Any approach to development must be underpinned by some sets of values and norms whether explicit or not. The human rights approach to development on an explicit framework of norms and values has been universally accepted and codified through different international Conventions, Treaties, Declarations and Covenants (Osmani, 2005). This approach adopts a particular view of what constitutes development, which has been best exemplified in 'the right to development'. 'The Right to development is an inalienable human rights by virtue of which every human being and all people are entitled to participate in, contribute to and enjoy economic, social, cultural and political development, in which all human rights and fundamental rights can be fully realised'[5].

The Declaration on the right to development also recognizes the close relationship between human rights and development that are needed to address the underlying causes of migration. Human Development is defined as a process of enlarging peoples' choices, of which the most critical one is to lead a long and healthy life, to be educated and to enjoy a decent standard of living (UNDP, HDR, 1990). The basic idea of human development—that enriching the lives and freedoms of ordinary people is fundamental—has much in common with the objects of human rights. The two are complementary. Human Rights and Human Development are thus close enough in motivation and concern is compatible and congruous, and they are different enough in strategy and design to complement each other fruitfully (UNDP, HDR, 2000). Both human rights and principle of equality assist development—by giving all members of society similar chances to be economically productive. Thus from a development perspective, greater equity in the long run underpins faster growth.

The Committee on Migrant Workers (CMW) has emphasized that full protection of human rights will remove many of the root causes of migration, such as violation of economic and social rights, discrimination and violence.[6] In this situation, policies, which protect and respect human rights, are not only legal duties for states, but also a means to the end of making migration a matter of choice. But less attention has been paid to the role of human rights during migration process or to the ways in which a lack of respect for human rights of migrant workers reduces their ability to contribute to the development. Human rights are central, not ancillary, to the migration-development process. The efforts, which respect human rights, goes far beyond the individual migrant, and benefit their home, societies and those in which they live and work. Migrants' ability to be productive and contribution to their own and their families' welfare, to the national economy through social security and tax contributions, and also to their home communities is directly related to their conditions of work. Similarly, the contribution is also conditioned by the migrants' integration in the country of settlement. Respect for the basic human rights of all persons in each society is an essential basis for addressing and resolving the tensions and potential conflicts between people who have different interests and socio-cultural backgrounds.

Contributions to development are more limited from communities in which most of the members have no secure legal status, are not incorporated in the formal labour market, do not get an education of equality—all these that make it likely that their resources will be meagre and largely absorbed by their daily survival needs. Rights based policies, which promote access to health care and adequate housing, training and language acquisition, will strengthen equality and build the capacity of diaspora communities to access labour market and lead productive, culturally and socially enriching lives. The Global Commission on International Migration (GCIM) also pointed out to the dangers associated with the social exclusion and marginalisation of migrants. It also noted that 'in the absence of effective integration, destination countries will not be able to capitalize on the contribution that migrants can make to the society'.[7] Thus, it is evident that there is a direct link between respect for human rights of migrants and greater—maximised development benefits from migration and conversely between a lack of respect for human rights and reduced—minimised development contribution by migrants.

Therefore, a human rights framework would contribute to migration policies through the acceptance of common basic principles. International co-operation and consultation should take place within this framework. The presence of sustained, participatory integration policies, and cooperation between source and destination countries are key factors in determining integration outcomes. Rights based policy-making should take into account the vulnerability of migrants and their human rights protection needs throughout the migration process. It should focus on the causes of migration and on the need to ensure respect for human rights in the countries from which most migrants originate. It must further reflect the vulnerability of all migrants—irregular as well as regular—recognize both the link between legal status and human rights and the negative correlation between irregularity of status and exploitation. In all situations, dispelling the myths that fuel discrimination and bolster xenophobia as well as promoting inter-cultural understanding is undoubtedly a step in the right direction. Unless migration is approached through this perspective, two difficulties arise: first and self evidently—that the protection of migrants' rights is not given priority; secondly, that where migration is seen only in economic terms, migrants may come to be regarded as commodities, rather than as individuals entitled to full enjoyment of human rights. In a world in which more and more people are on the move, ignoring migrants' rights would seriously jeopardise the welfare, not only of migrants, but also of all human beings.

NOTES

1. The Migrant Population in the UK: fiscal effects, Home Office RDS Occasional Paper No. 77, 2002, p. 11.
2. CERD General Recommendation No. 30 # 34.
3. UNESCO (available at *www.unesco.org/migration*).
4. The six core UN Conventions are:
5. See Article-1 of the Declaration on the Right to Development, 1986.
6. CMW/C/4/CRP.2, para 4.
7. GCIM, supra, p. 45.

REFERENCES

Awases, M., *et al.* (2004): *Migration of Health Professionals in Six Countries: A Synthesis*, p. 40. Brazzaville, Congo: World Health Organization Regional Office for Africa.

GCIM (2005): *Migration in an Interconnected World: New Directions for Action: Report of the Global Commission on International Migration*, p. 36. Geneva: Global Commission on International Migration.

HDR (2000): *Human Development Report*, p. 17: UNDP.

ICMW (2003): UN International Convention on the Protection of the Rights of All Migrant Workers and Members of their Families (2003). Part-III.

ILO (2004): *Towards a Fair Deal for Migrant Workers in the global economy*, para. 126.

Lonnroth, Juhani (1991): 'The International Convention on the Rights of All Migrants and Members of their Families in the Context of International Migration Policies: An Analysis of Ten Years of Negotiation', in *International Migration Review* 25(4): 710-736.

Lowell, B. L. A. Findlay, and E. Stewart (2004): "Brain Strain: Optimising Highly Skilled Migration from Developing Countries," p. 9, Asylum and Migration Working Paper. No. 3. London: Institute for Public Policy Research. Web site: *www.ippr.org/ecomm/files/brainstrain.pdf*

Osmani, S.R. (2005): 'Globalisation and Human Rights Approach to Development'. The Paper was presented on the occasion of 60th Session of the Commission on Human Rights, organized by the Office of High Commissioner on Human Rights in Geneva during 9-10 February, 2004.

TARAN, Patrick A. (2000a). 'Human Rights of Migrants: Challenges of the New Decade' in *International Migration* 38(6): 7-51.

The World Bank (2006). *Global Economic Prospects 2006: Economic Implications of Remittances and Migration*, pp. 85 and 88. Washington, D.C.: The International Bank for Reconstruction and Development and the World Bank.

Thouez, C. (2005). *The Impact of Remittances on Development*. pp. 41-52 in UNFPA 2005.

UNDP (1990): *Human Development Report 1990*, pp. 9-10.

UNDP (2000): *Human Development Report 2000*, p. 19.

UNFPA (2006): UNFPA State of World Report 2006: A Passage to Hope, Women and International Migration. Web Site: *www.unfpa.org*

UNHCR (2006a). *2005 Global Refugee Trends: Statistical Overview of Populations of Refugees, Asylum-Seekers, Internally Displaced Persons, Stateless Persons, and Other Persons of Concern to UNHCR*, p. 3. Geneva: UNHCR.

UNHCR (2006b): *The State of the World's Refugees 2006: Human Displacement in the New Millennium*, p. 70. Oxford, United Kingdom, and New York: Oxford University Press.

United Nations (2006a): *Trends in Total Migrant Stock: The 2005 Revision: CD-ROM Documentation* (POP/DB/MIG/Rev.2005/Doc). New York: Population Division, Department of Economic and Social Affairs, United Nations.

United Nations (2006b). *World Population Monitoring, Focusing on International Migration and Development: Report of the Secretary-General* (E/CN.9/2006/3).

Section Four

Human Development in the Context of Human Resource Development

9

Human Resource Allocation and Education-Employment Trade-Offs

SHRI PRAKASH

Introduction: Decision Variable(s) of Allocation

Family is the basic decision-making unit at micro level. The basic decisions are conventionally supposed to relate to allocation of income between consumption and investment. Both investment and consumption depend upon disposable income of households. Income, in its turn, depends on the resources which individual households are endowed with. The household's resource endowments may broadly be divided into: (1) land, (2) buildings and other forms of income yielding real estate and assets, (3) capital, and (4) labour.

In the non-communist capitalist economics, means of production and income yielding assets are distributed unevenly among different segments of society. Distribution of resources like land, capital and other forms of wealth is highly skewed. The poor are endowed merely with low level human resources as the means of earnings.

In case of poor or not so rich families, allocation of family labour between economically productive and non-productive activities emerges as the core allocation decision to determine family incomes. This study attempts to analyse the choice making aspects of behaviour of households endowed exclusively with labour as an instrument of income generation. Naturally, allocation choices relate mainly to the allocation of family labour between different activities.

Activities attracting labour allocation decision may be divided into following broad categories:

(i) Productive activities for income generation
(ii) Education
(iii) Domestic chores, and
(iv) Cultural, leisure and pleasure activities.

Last two activities may be grouped together for reducing decision variables by one. Major proportion of income of households of low occupation-income-social strata is accounted by wage incomes. There is hardly any unearned component in these household's incomes. Wage incomes may accrue either through self-employment or wage employment. The low wage/income employment of either variety is concentrated mostly in the unorganised and informal sectors of the economy.

Education and Income Interrelation

The mechanism of accumulation of human capital through investment in education is vicious in nature. Persons currently employed in low income and low-wage occupations in the informal and unorganised sectors of the economy have been born in poor households. Consequently, their parents could not afford the investment in education and training needed for high income-wage occupations. The parental no/low skill, low/no capital base has deprived these persons as children an access to education and skills, pushing them to occupations requiring no or low education, training and skills. Thus, the want of education, training and skills forced these people into current employment in less prestigious and low wage/income occupations. Low wage employment leads to low income which, in turn, leads to higher supply of labour for employment in low-wage-low-skill-no education occupations. This, in turn, leads to poverty. Poverty, in its turn, leads to no/low demand for education. This has naturally kept their incomes low. Their low incomes, in turn, now force them to keep their own children out of schools. This constitutes the vicious circle of low income-no-education-low wage employment and illiteracy[1]. This vicious circle manifests an in-built mechanism of inter-generational transference of economic and educational inequalities (Prakash, 1977, 1995 ; Myrdal, 1958). Out of school children belong mostly to the families of these low income-education-occupation groups.

Out of school children of this group may be classified into two categories: (i) those who never went to any school, and (ii) those who joined school but left without completing primary/middle education. Nearly 75 per cent of all droppers from elementary education are the droppers from first three classes of primary education (Prakash, 1993). Approximately 36 per cent of all out of school children are employed (Prakash and Debal, 1994). Children who have never gone to school or are early school droppers may either be (i) poor academic performers with weak economic base, and/or (ii) good academic performers with weak economic base (Prakash, 1989).

Most children from poor households do not perform well in schools. Even if they perform well, the poor parents often withdraw them from schools at the first available job opportunity. Twin factors affect withdrawal decisions: (i) even if the children perform well, it may be beyond the means of the parents to afford schooling of children upto high or higher secondary levels. The completion of primary or middle education does not command any differential earnings or job opportunities in the labour market. The primary or middle education does not serve as an instrument of access to any specific occupations/ jobs in the labour market, (ii) primary and middle education is not relevant to the jobs available for employment to these children, (iii) whereas jobs requiring high or higher secondary education may be difficult to obtain by these children after the completion of that level of education, the low-wage-low-occupation jobs, needing no education, become easily available to them even without primary education. Besides, the need for supplementation of family incomes by the earnings of these children is felt acutely by such households, making the opportunity cost of education to such families, measured by foregone earnings, unaffordable (Prakash and Chaubey, 1992). Therefore, the process of dropping-out may occur at the very first job opportunity that becomes available. This enhances demand for employment which, in turn, depresses the demand for education at low family incomes, facilitating the substitution of employment for education.

The substitution process, however, gets reversed at higher stages of education. Once a child has completed elementary education, he/ she is practically lost to the world of blue collar work. After the completion of elementary education, most children aspire for more prestigious white collar jobs, needing at least secondary education.

This operationalises the ratchet process and releases the impulses of demonstration effect on educational demand. This makes education its own cause. Then, the completion of high and higher secondary education leaves the large majority of students with the choice between immediate unemployment or further education, leading to the substitution of education for employment (Prakash, 1989). Thus, at this end of education-employment spectrum, substitution process gets reversed.

Superior-Inferior Goods Dichotomy

Basic goods, essential for existence of physical health of a man, are food, clothing and shelter. But along with these goods, education, culture and ideology are also essential ingredients in the basic goods basket for mental health and higher quality of life (*Cf.* Robinson, 1964, *Cf.* Afxentiou, 1994). For the rural and urban poor of India, education may rank only fourth or fifth in order of priority after food, clothing, shelter and medicines needed for health. This group of commodities constitutes the necessities of physical survival. Education of children may either be luxury, or at best, a convenience. It is a superior good in either case[2]. Education, however, leads to the building of competencies and capabilities of man. Hence, investment of time, labour, money and other resources in education leads to the raising of potential earnings/incomes. During post Second World War period, education has, in fact, emerged as the focal point of socio-economic development on this count (Schultz, 1962).

General Equilibrium Framework of Allocation Model

The demand for education and demand for employment are highly inter-related. Wage income depends upon the nature of occupation and the sector of economy in which one is employed. This study, therefore, attempts to develop a simple general equilibrium type input output model for explaining the choice making aspects of behaviour of poor households.

Human Resource Allocation Model

Allocation of human resources among three activities may be represented by an Input-Output Transaction Matrix:

To/From	*Activities*			
Resource	*Education*	*Economic Work*	*Domestic Work*	*Total*
Children	X (11)	X (12)	X (13)	X (1)
Males	X (21)	X (22)	X (23)	X (2)
Females	X (31)	X (32)	X (33)	X (3)
Total	X (1)	X (2)	X (3)	X (x)

where $x\ (ij)$ denotes units of i-th human resource allocated to j-th activity and ij = 1, 2, 3 are subscripts indexing resource type and activities. Subscript 1 refers to children as resources, adult males and females are indexed by human resource 2 and 3 respectively. Correspondingly, education constitutes resource use for future income generation and it is indexed as activity 1, while current income generation and domestic activities, including leisure and pleasure activities, are indexed by subscripts 2 and 3 respectively. It is assumed that x (1), x (2) and x (3) are total quantities of three types of human resources respectively. It is also assumed that allocation of resources among three activities exactly exhaust available supplies:

$$x(1) = x(11) + x(12) + x(13) \quad (1)$$
$$x(2) = x(21) + x(22) + x(23) \quad (2)$$
$$x(3) = x(31) + x(32) + x(33) \quad (3)$$

Balance equations may, however, be transformed into structural equations:

$$[a(11) + a(12) + a(13)]\, x(1) = x(1)$$
$$[a(21) + a(22) + a(23)]\, x(2) = x(2)$$
$$[a(31) + a(32) + a(33)]\, x(3) = x(3)$$

Obviously, $a(ij) = x(ij)/x(i)$ are the allocation coefficients that conceptually differ from technologically determined coefficients of conventional input-output models[3]. Total human resources allocated to each activity may then be derived by the transposition of above equations:

$$a(11)\, x(1) + a(21)\, x(2) + a(31)\, x(3) = x(1) \quad (4)$$
$$a(12)\, x(1) + a(22)\, x(2) + a(32)\, x(3) = x(2) \quad (5)$$
$$a(13)\, x(1) + a(23)\, x(2) + a(33)\, x(3) = x(3) \quad (6)$$
$$A'x = X \quad (7)$$

where $A' = [a(ji)]$, x and X are vectors of available supply and quantities of allocation of human resources to different activities. Allocation coefficients will, however, be determined in this study as behavioural probabilities/propensities. There is 1 degree of freedom which can be used to specify either vector x or vector X; A, the matrix of allocation coefficients, like technology matrix A of input output models, is assumed to be known. Equation 7 assumes x to be known to determine X. If X is known, then x can be determined as follows:

$$x = [A^1]^{-1} X = [A^{-1}]' X.$$

Human Resource Allocation to Income Generation Activities

Human resources required for productive work depend upon the income desired by the family for consumption. Depending upon adequacy or inadequacy of earnings of male adults, one, two or all three human resources may be required to be allocated to productive work[4]. It is assumed that income needs are the first charge on adult human resources. Low income groups which this analysis focuses on allocated all adult members of the family to labour market. Merely wages at which adult males and females of this group work warrant that. Male and female wage rates are, however, assumed to be known. It is also assumed that domestic activities constitute the residual charge on human resources of the households. These assumptions facilitate determination of (i) income of adult members of the family exogenously, on the one hand, and (ii) labour to household chores residually, on the other.

Desired or planned income is governed, by and large, by expenditure required for meeting the consumption needs:

$$Y^* (ijt) = f\{C(ijt)\} \tag{9}$$

where Y^* is desired income and C is consumption.

Consumption is generally treated as the function of prices and income, given the family size. Prices enter as the decisive determinants of demand/consumption of individual commodities. In the determination of aggregate national or household consumption, prices loose much of their weight. Number of consumer units or family size and income are important determinants in such cases. Larger the family size, greater will be the consumption expenditure and smaller the family size, lower will be the consumption expenditure. Consumption expenditure will be directly related to family size. Measurement of both dependent and independent variables on per capita basis will eliminate family size from the equation as an explicit determinant of consumption. However, consumption of particular goods of given quality over prolonged periods converges towards habits, tastes and preferences, making consumption levels downward sticky and irreversible. It is, therefore, assumed that the preceding period's consumption constitutes the minimum consumption needs which may be taken as the committed part of total consumption (*Cf.* Stone, 1954). Alternatively, preceding period's consumption may be brought into the model as the determinant either through partial adjustment hypothesis or adaptative expectation model.

The downward irreversibility of consumption does not imply absence of upward flexibility. Levels and patterns of expenditure are indeed highly flexible upwards. In a dynamically growing economy, numerous persons move from lower to next higher income group(s) each year. All new entrants from lower income brackets into higher income groups imitate the living styles of the peer group into which they move. The process of adaptation to the levels and patterns of consumption of higher income groups into which the households move from lower income groups may be spread over several periods. Influence of this demonstration effect may be captured by the peer group's average consumption expenditure. The average expenditure of the group will, however, constitute the floor to which new entrants aspire to rise at the earliest. The ceiling of the new consumption expenditure level will depend upon the additional income of the household that has facilitated its entry into new higher income group.

The consumption function may, therefore, be specified as follows:

$$C(ijt) = f[\Delta Y(ij), C(ijt\text{-}1), G(ijt)] \qquad (10)$$

Where $\Delta Y(ijt)$ denotes additional income and G represents average expenditure of the peer group. Substitution of C(*ijt*) from (10) into (9) will facilitate the determination of $Y^*(ijt)$, whereas $Y(jit)$, actual household income of adults, will be given by the product of known adult wage rates and the quantity of adult human resources:

$$w(2)\, x\, (ij2) + w(3)\, x\, (ij3) = Y\, (ijt) \qquad (11)$$

where w(2) and $w(3)$ are male and female wage rates, $Y(ijt)$ is actual income of i-th household of j-th group at time t that is generated by employment of all adult human resources. Aggregation over households and groups will yield estimates of total adult income. But x (21), x (31), $x(23)$ and $x(33)$ may be measured separately in man-hours devoted to educational and domestic activities. Adult males and females have an obligation of income generation for meeting family needs. Only such labour and man-hours are allocated to education and domestic work as are left after the discharge of economic activities. Therefore, $x(21)$ and $x(31)$ will be determined independently on separate principles. As a first approximation, these man-hours and labour are assumed to be known. Models for their determination can, however, be developed easily.

The main objectives of the study is to determine $x(11)$ and $x(12)$ in terms of behavioural propensities. Determination of these two unknowns of the system warrants the knowledge of $x(22)$ and $x(32)$; but $x(12)$ depends on the extent of the need for supplementation of family incomes by children's earnings and $x(11)$ will depend upon the private demand for education which is also related to income requirements from child labour, on the one hand, and household income of adults, on the other. Allocation of children to labour market will obviously be determined by the gap between the desired and adult income of the household. Given the child wage rate $w(1)\, x\, (12)$ will be determined by

$$x(12) = [Y(*) - Y]/w(1) \qquad (12)$$

where $[Y(*) - Y]$ is obviously the total income gap to be filled up by the earnings of child workers. Determination of allocation of children to education is considered separately in the ensuing analysis.

As a consumer good, education can be treated as the direct function of price. If education is a normal good, demand will be an inverse function of price. If education is a superior good, educational demand will vary directly both with income and price of educational service. Private cost under consumption approach to educational demand will have current and future consumption benefits for comparison with cost as is the case with all consumer goods. As current and future consumption benefits are mostly non-momentary in nature, satisfaction of utility is generally the entity of comparison. $C(b)/U(*)$ will denote the demand price of education as an investment good only with respect to the denominator. Investment approach collapses cost and earnings into cost-benefit ratio as educational investment. Conventional theory of consumer behaviour assumes that the demand for a good will be pushed up to the point where utility equals price. Investment theory of education postulates equalisation of cost and earnings in equilibrium, facilitating elimination of the variable in the denominator of the price. For equilibrium analysis, consideration of the numerator of these two demand prices may suffice, leading to the collapsing of two demand functions into one as the same demand price will then enter as the determinant of demand in both these functions. Tastes and preferences, private disposable income and age-specific population size will constitute the shift parameters of this demand function (Prakash and Chowdhury, 1993). The demand function is specified as follows:

$$E(d) = f[C(b), Y(d), N(a)]$$

where $E(d)$ is educational demand (total enrolments) $C(b)$ denotes total private cost/expenditure on education, $Y(d)$ shows total private disposal income, and $N(a)$ is total age-specific population. Theoretically education specific age-population will constitute the upper limit of demand for places in institutions.

Stochastic Nature of Educational Demand

Decision to acquire education endows the person with the attribute of being educated. The consequence of this behavioural decision is attributional. It is not certain *a priori* whether an individual household will enter education market as its buyer. Therefore, stochastic rather than deterministic functional specification will be warranted under conditions of uncertainty. Numerous households, having low-income-occupation profiles prefer their children to work rather than learn. The risk involved is that the decision is irreversible since such children may not be able to re-enter formal education after crossing certain age. Then, they will have to remain in occupations with lower earnings for ever. Substitution of work for education involves the risk of remaining in low-income occupation for ever and uncertainty of higher income jobs ever becoming accessible without education. Availability of any job, leave apart the desired job, is not certain under conditions of unemployment. Impending unemployment may prompt numerous students to enter or stay in higher education, delaying entry into labour market. The decision-maker will still bear the risk of remaining unemployed for some time or getting even after completing next higher stage of education a job available to people with lower education. Substitution of education for work involves not only opportunity cost but also a certain degree of uncertainty and risk of the above type.

Other choices and substitution possibilities operate with regard to the type of educational institution, its spatial location, and the type of studies to be prosecuted (Prakash, 1979; Prakash and Chowdhury, 1992; *Cf.* Pscharopoulos and Soumelis, 1979). These choices and substitution possibilities lead to uncertain situations and outcomes. If places supplied by educational institutions either exceed or equal users' demand and the patterns of their aspirations, there will be no unsatisfied demand at each level and type of education. There exist institutions having open-door admission policy while other institutions may pursue restrictive admission policy. Numerous devices of screening and filtering the aspirants are used for the purpose.[5] Irreversibility of choices exercised and their uncertain outcomes regarding choice of (a) institution, (b) its spatial location, and (c) subject(s) of study are minimised by the pursuit of admission into alternative institutions/locations/subjects. In case of non-availability of higher preferences, parents and their wards choose even the least desired option rather than to go without education. These uncertainties of available options warrant the adoption of stochastic rather than deterministic model. Division of (13) by N(a) will yield such specification.

$$\frac{Ed}{N(a)} = f[1/N(a)\ \{C(b),\ Y(d)\}] \tag{14}$$

For obviating both conceptual and data problems, denominators of *C(b)* and *Y(d)* in (14) may be replaced by actual enrolments and total population respectively to yield:

$$p = f(c, y) \tag{15}$$

where $p = E(d)$ is an individual's probability of being enrolled in an institution, and $c = C(b)/E(d)$ is the unit price/cost, $E(d)$ is total enrolments, and $y = Y(d)/N$ is per capita disposable income.

There exists a threshold income for activating formal educational demand. Threshold income defines the affordability of cost/price of education. If actual income exceeds the threshold level at which price of education is affordable, an individual will be enrolled. Let the choice variable be denoted by $r(ij)$, then $r(ij) = 1$ if $y > = y(0)$ where $y = m\, y(0)$ and $m > = 1$, and $r(Ij) = 0$ if $m < 1$.

Thus, decision variable r(ij) will emerge as binary in nature, admitting 1 and 0 as its values. The sampled households may be classified into several groups according to income that guides allocation decisions. The sampled households will form S distinct income groups. For group j, having $n(j)$ households, all households, characterised by $r(ij) = 1$, may be aggregated so that total households with this attribute are $S(j)$. Similarly, all households, having $r(ij) = 0$, are aggregated to yield the sum $K(j)$ of such households, where $S(j) + K(j) = n(j)$, $p(j) = S(j)/n(j)$ and $p(j)$ is the probability of an individual of j-th income group being enrolled in education. The corresponding value of non-enrolment probability will be $q(j) = 1 - p(j)$. Given the value of enrolment probability, allocation of children to education may be determined as follows:

$$X(11) = Px \tag{16}$$

where $X(11)$ is the column vector of children enrolled in each state, P is the diagonal matrix of probabilities of enrolment and x is the column vector of child population of 6-14 year age groups. The enrolment probabilities will pertain only 6-14 year age group children.

Empirical Prognostication of the Model

A variety of data are required for empirical prognostication of the model. Data limitations have forced certain proximate assumptions and treatment of particular variables of the model as exogenous or endogenous. In view of above limitations and constraints, only $x(11)$ and x (12) have been determined within the model. Quinquennial NSS Survey of 1988-89 has been used as the data base for age, state and income-wise enrolments and non-enrolments of 6-14 year age group children in schools. Reports on working children, cited as references, have been used for determining child workers and their wages. Data relating to per capita income of states have been taken from Economic Survey. Almost all the results based on model calculations, however, pertain to 1992-93.

Each sub-model has been prognosticated empirically with the above data base in accordance with the procedures and inter-relations between the endogenous and exogenous variables of these sub-models. Estimates of enrolment probabilities and income elasticity of consumption have been used to work out allocation coefficients. Results of each sub-model are discussed in details in the ensuing analysis.

Operational Results for Employment-Education Allocation Sub-Models

Allocation of children to education has been determined by equation (16) whereas estimates of Y^* have been derived from experiments with aggregate consumption function of equation (10). Consumption estimates have yielded desired levels of income. Observed per capita

Model Estimates

States	*Population (6-14 years old)*	*Child Workers*	*Non-Enrollees*	*Enrollees*	*Observed Enrolment Probabilities*	*Enrolment Probabilities*
Arunachal Pradesh	11211700	1952573	3200940	8010760	0.838	0.7145
Assam	5067800	1208615	1702274	3365526	0.885	0.6641
Bihar	16618200	627553	6477774	10140426	0.7504	0.6102
Haryana	3023300	198204	600618	260682	0.9858	0.8125
Madhya Pradesh	12150100	1828346	4155334	7994766	0.7497	0.6580
Rajasthan	9107800	1657073	3012860	6094940	0.7435	0.6692
Gujarat	7317900	224630	1871918	544982	0.9597	0.7442
Karnataka	8326600	1619923	2382240	5944360	0.8438	0.7139
Maharashtra	12940800	1304433	2608865	10331935	0.9448	0.7984
Orissa	5623600	731484	1924958	3698642	0.8329	0.6577
West Bengal	11694700	1914282	3418360	8276340	0.7946	0.7077
Tamil Nadu	9157000	1528532	2779149	6377851	0.9553	0.6965
Punjab	3374600	336359	551409	2823191	0.9617	0.8366

income of the states has been adjusted for the earnings of working children in order to estimate income per adult. Estimated gaps between desired and actual income have furnished expected amount of income to be generated from the earnings of children. Income gaps have been used to determine the number of children required to work for supplementing family incomes. The child workers constitute the major proportion of total non-enrollees among the children of 6-14 year age groups. The model estimates of these unknown variables, determined within the system, are reported.

Model estimates are quite satisfactory in so far as the error margins of the forecasted values are low. Thus, the model has been found to be operationally feasible though the accuracy of predictions can be raised by improvements in the quality of data base.

Empirical Experiments with Education Sub-Model

A composite hypothesis has been proposed in the study in order to identify the true determinants of demand or want of demand for education. Enrolment represents effective demand for education whereas non-enrolment may, as a corollary, be construed to denote the want of demand for education. Educational demand has been postulated as the function of income and cost, including opportunity cost:

$$P(j) = f[c(j), y(j)] \qquad (17)$$

where $p(j)$ is enrolment probability of children of j-th income group, $c(j)$ is unit cost and $y(j)$ is per capita income of group j.

Non-Enrolment Proposition

As the first approximation, the hypothesis that low income makes high educational price unaffordable is proposed. Low income leads to reduction or even elimination of demand for education. Lower demand for education implies low enrolment and high non-enrolment probability. Similarly, higher price of education is expected to lead to lower enrolment and higher non-enrolment probabilities. Non-enrolment probabilities may, therefore, be postulated as an inverse function of income and/or price:

$$\text{Log } q(j) = \log a + b \log y(j) \tag{18}$$

Alternatively, linear functional form may be specified:

$$Q(j) = a + b\, y(j) \tag{19}$$

where q is the probability of non-enrolment. The experimental nature of investigations suggest the testing of multi-variety functional forms for empirical validation:

$$q = Y b + u$$

where Y is the matrix of the values of independent variables. This may also need modification in order to take cognizance of the grouped nature of observations. The model may be reformulated as follows:

$$q = Y M b + u$$

where M is the matrix of frequencies of q, Y values. These models may be defined as linear probability models.

The functions have been estimated from grouped data for which computational procedure is detailed below:

$$q = 1/n\, \Sigma\, q\, f(q) \tag{20}$$
$$y = 1/n\, \Sigma\, y\, f(y) \tag{21}$$
$$S^2(q) = 1/n\, \Sigma q^2 f(q) - q^2 \tag{22}$$
$$S^2(y) = 1/n\, \Sigma y^2 f(y) - y^2 \tag{23}$$
$$S(qy) = 1/n\, \Sigma\, qy\, f(qy) - q\, y \tag{24}$$

Regression parameters can then be estimated in the usual way. OLS estimates of regression equations (18) and (19), based on grouped data, are reported below:

$$\text{Log } q(j) = 5.082 - 1.214 \log y(j) \qquad r^2 = 0.4173,\ t = -6.44$$
$$Q(j) = 4.386 - 0.0024\, y(j) \qquad r^2 = 0.3568,\ t = -5.67$$

The regression and correlation coefficients of both linear and log-linear forms are highly significant statistically. Explained proportion of variation in non-enrolment probabilities range from 36 to 42 per cent. Besides, income elasticity of non-enrolment probability and the coefficient of marginal change have negative signs, implying that the probability of non-enrolment and average household income are inversely related. Thus, these results lend credence and furnish empirical validity to the hypothesis underlying the model tested herein.

These results indirectly substantiate the corollary of the hypothesis that the probability of enrolment is the direct function of income. Conventionally, demand is postulated as the direct function of income and as an inverse function of price. Price of education, however, differs from the usual concept of price. In case of other goods and services, the price that consumer pays and the price that producer receives are the same.

Unit Educational Cost

Education involves both direct and indirect costs. Direct cost of education is accounted by user charges, uniforms, transport, books and stationary. Expenditure incurred on education per child by the family may be defined as the private unit cost/price of education. Even though user charges may be the same for all students in the same institution, these differ from institution to institution. Relatively richer segments of population send their children to high fee charging private institutions, whereas poorer segments admit their wards in no or low fee charging government institutions. Quality differentials of learning-teaching processes reflect the differential user prices. Expenses on such items as uniforms and transport may vary with the bearing/paying capacity. It may, therefore, be hypothesised that unit cost or user price is directly related to income.

Compulsory education commands zero market price. Institutions for higher education may fix user charges below cost. Educational subsidies may range from zero to hundred per cent which the producer of education receives as direct grants from the government. Then, payments made for books and stationery, uniforms and transport do not accrue to the educational producers while fees may constitute only a fraction of private cost of education, on the one hand, and these may cover only negligible proportion of institutional cost (Prakash, 1977). But more often that not, quality differentials of education service are much more highly marked than the quality differentials characterising material goods. Most consumers prefer demand for places in educational institutions which supply high quality education though their user charges may be correspondingly high. It is because of this facet of education that we find capacity utilization in government schools to be low while there is a great pressure on the limited capacities of high fee charging private institutions. In view of this, enrolment probability and unit price of education are postulated to be directly related. If enrolment probability is postulated to be a function of both income and unit price, the model may be extended as follows:

$$p = Yb + gC + u$$

where C is matrix of values of unit price of education. Log linear forms of above functions can easily be specified as alternatives.

High income-high price nexus may reflect inferior-superior good syndrome of education as an item of expenditure. Low incomes lead to choice of lower quality and low price institutions. The OLS estimates of linear and log linear functional forms to test the nature of relationship between income and price are reported below:

$$c = 211.9621 + 0.0533\,y \qquad r^2 = 0.3674,\ t = 2.53$$
$$\log c = 0.3798 + 0.6192 \log y \qquad r^2 = 0.4188,\ t = 2.02$$

where y is per capita income and c is expenditure on education per student.

Regression and correlation coefficients have the predicted signs and both are statistically significant.

Marginal propensity to consume/spend on education indicates that an increase of 1 rupee worth of income leads to an increase of 5 paisa in cost/price of education, while income elasticity of cost highlights the fact that the doubling of income leads to 62 per cent increase in the price paid for education. These results validate the hypothesis that income and educational price/cost are directly related. This makes educational price move directly with demand. Higher the price, greater will be educational demand. But opportunity cost constitutes the largest proportion of cost of education while educational demand varies inversely with foregone earnings. The presence of both these variables as the determinants of enrolment or non-enrolment probabilities may lead to multi-collinearity. This proposition will be examined directly.

Probability Model and Its Variants

OLS estimates of linear probability model and its variants are reported below:

$$p = 67.1421 + 0.0034\, y \qquad r^2 = 0.6006,\ t = 4.07$$
$$\log p = 1.837 + 0.00002\, y \qquad r^2 = 0.5900,\ t = 3.97$$
$$\log p = 1.0486 + 0.2377 \log y \qquad r^2 = 0.6173,\ t = 4.21$$

Linear changes in per capita income explain three-fifths of total variations of enrolment probability. Regression and correlation coefficients are positive and statistically significant. Semi-log variant of the function furnishes similar estimates though it explains only 58.9 per cent of total changes in enrolment probability. Estimates of log-linear variant of probability model show that the changes in per capita income explain 62 per cent of total changes in enrolment probability, highlighting its highest explanatory power. The value of statistically significant income elasticity coefficient of enrolment probability is only 0.24, implying that any given change in income evokes only one-fourth of its own magnitude as change in enrolment probability. Thus, log-linear probability (LLP) version emerges as the most satisfactory model on statistical grounds.

Theoretically, enrolment probability has been postulated to be the direct function of income and unit educational price. Hence, all above variants of probability model furnish only partial validation of the composite hypothesis.

Since predicted values of p are expected to remain within the range of 0 and 1 as per capita income reaches extremely high/low levels, Logit model suggest itself as an appropriate alternative. Otherwise, the predicted values may fall beyond the prescribed range for larger/smaller values of the determinants of enrolment probability. In view of this, price/cost has not been introduced as the second determinant in above models. Instead of this, bi-variety and multiple Logit models have been tried. The OLS estimates of the Logit function of the enrolment probabilities are reported below:

$$\log (p/q) = 0.631 + 0.0002\, y \qquad r^2 = 0.6478,\ t = 4.50$$

Obviously, Logit model emerges to be the better functional relation than all other functions considered earlier. Explained proportion of variation furnished by Logit happens to be the highest though value of r^2 is not a very satisfactory criterion in case of Logit functions. Unit educational price is introduced as an additional determinant of enrolment probability in Logit model to evaluate the thesis that educational demand is a function of income and price. OLS estimates of the function are given below:

$$\log (p/q) = -0.1379 + 0.0002\, y + 0.0004\, c$$
$$t\,(3.10),\ (0.001)\ R^2 = 0.6604$$

Above estimates show that (1) introduction of educational price brings negligible improvement in the explanatory power of the bivariate function, revealing educational price as superfluous determinant of enrolment probability, (2) though the sign and significance of the coefficient of income in the function have not changed as a consequence of introduction of educational price as the second determinant, the function is still afflicted by multi collinearity. This proposition will be further evaluated rigorously, and (3) educational unit price has been acting as the proxy of income when income is absent as an explicit determinant in the functional relation. Last two propositions have been found empirically valid.

$$(\log Z^{GLS}) = 3.5121 + .000\,00004\ Y \quad R^2 = 0.7712,\ t = 6.09$$

where Z and Y are the variables of logit model transformed by the variance of p. A comparison of Logit with empirical estimates of other functions substantiates the theoretical expectation that Logit model is superior in such cases. Even though OLS is valid for estimating logit models of this type (Hebden, 1983), GLS estimates are superior on theoretical grounds. OLS estimates of time series models may be transformed into GLS estimates through auto-regression while OLS estimates of cross-section models may be transformed into GLS estimates through auto-regression while OLS estimates of cross-section models may be immunised from hcteroscadasticity by appropriate adjustment of variables. But the explained proportion of variation in general and in case of estimates of Logit models in particular may be inappropriate criterion of choice between alternative functional forms or estimation procedures. GLS estimates of the Logit function, however, emerge to be best in this respect also. It will, therefore, be reasonable to select GLS estimates of the Logit function for the determination of sub allocation models in this study.

The OLS estimates of Logit model have been evaluated by White Test (Kmenta, 1972) for the presence of heteroscedasticity. White Test is based on the comparison of the sample variance of least square estimates under conditions of homoscedasticity and under conditions of heteroscedasticity. If the hypothesis holds true, estimates of two variances in large samples will differ due only to sampling fluctuations. The test equation is given below:

$$u^2(i) = a(0) + a(1)\, z(i1) + a(2)\, z(i2) + \ldots\ldots + a(p)\, z(ip) + e(i)$$

where $u(i)$ is the error of OLS estimates. Coefficient of determination of this function is designated as $R^2(w)$. Under null hypothesis of homoscedasticity, $nR^2(w) \approx \chi^2(p)$ asymptotically. For example bivariate regression model, White sets $p = 2$, $z(it) = x(i)$ and $z(i2) = x^2(i)$ where x is explanatory variable. The test does not require specification of the form of heteroscedasticity.

OLS estimates of $u^2(i) = a(0) + a(1)\, z(i1) + a(2)\, z^2(i1)$ are reported below:

$$u^2(\text{i}) = -0.1774 + 0.0001\, z(i1) - 0.000001\, \text{z}(\text{-il})^2$$

$$t \qquad (1.14) \qquad (-1.04)$$

$$\chi^2(p) = 1.874 < 5.941 = \chi(\text{-}05), \qquad R^2 = 0.1442$$

In this case, heteroscedasticity does not emerge as serious as it has been expected on *a priori* grounds. Therefore, OLS estimates of the Logit model may be as valid as GLS ones on this consideration.

Conclusions and Resume

The input-output type allocation model, developed with a view to empirically prognosticate it, has been found to be empirically valid. The behavioural input-output coefficients of this model have been determined through hierarchical sub-models designed to determine these coefficients as behavioural propensities. The stochastic sub-models of the system developed for determining behavioural propensities have furnished reasonable results. The two most important behavioural parameters, determined within the system, are enrolment/non-enrolment probabilities and the propensity to participate in work force. Variety of experiments have, however, been conducted. Results establish that GLS estimates of Logit model rather than linear or log linear probability models furnish more reasonable and dependable results. OLS estimates of Logit model are not inferior to those yielded by GLS.

REFERENCES

Afxentiou, P.C. (1994). Basic Needs, Subsistence and Government, *The Indian Economic Journal*, Vol. 41, No. 4.

Bardhan, P. (1979). "Labour Supply Function in a Poor Agarian Economy," *American Economic Review*, Vol. 69, No. 1, pp. 73-83.

Dingwaney, Manjari *et al.* (1988). *Children of Darkness: A Manual on Child Labour in India*. Academy of Gandhian Studies, Hyderabad.

Ghosh, A. (1964). *Experiments with Input-Output Models*, Cambridge University Press, Massachusettes.

Hebden, Julia (1983). *Applications of Econometrics*, Philip Allen, Deddington, Oxford.

Intriligator, M.D. (1978). *Econometric Models, Techniques and Applications*, Prentice Hall of India, New Delhi.

Khandker, S.R. (1988). "Determinants of Women's Time Allocation in Rural Bangladesh," *Economic Development and Cultural Change*, Vol. 37, No. 1, pp. 111-126.

Kmenta, January (1986). *Elements of Econometrics*, Macmillan Publishing Co., New York.

Malathi, N. (1991). Some Aspects of Women Participation in Rural Labour Market of Pondicherry Region, Unpublished M.Phil. Dissertation, Pondicherry University, Pondicherry.

Myrdal, Gunnar (1958). *Economic Theory and Underdeveloped Regions*, Vora, Bombay.

N.S.S.O. (1989, 1994). A Report on Education and Literacy in India, 42nd and 47th Rounds, Government of India, Department of Statistics, New Delhi.

Nangia, Parveen and Panicker-Pinto, Rita (1988). Situation Analysis of Children in Specially Difficult Circumstances in the Union Territory of Delhi, A Report for UNICEF.

Nirmala, V. and Kamaiah B. (1993). "Labour Supply Behaviour of Wives with Living Spouse in Pondicherry," *Manpower Journal*, Vol. XXIX, No. 1, pp. 21-37.

Prakash, Shri (1977). *Educational System of India: An Econometric Study*, Concept, New Delhi.

Prakash, Shri (1989). Historical and Analytical Perspectives of Educational Planning in India, *Mimeographed* J.L. Nehru Centenary Conference on Four Decades of Development, NIEPA, New Delhi.

Prakash, Shri (1993). Universalisation of Elementary Education in India: Problems and Prospects, *Journal of Education and Social Change*, Vol. VII, No. 3.

Prakash, Shri and Chaubey, P.K. (1992). Universalisation of Education: A Simple General Equilibrium Type Policy Model, *Manpower Journal*, Vol. XXVIII.

Prakash, Shri and Chowdhury, Sumitra (1992). Private Demand for Education: A Probabilistic Approach, *Manpower Journal*, Vol. XXVIII, No.4, January-March.

Prakash, Shri and Debal, Praba (1994). Demographic and Social Accounting as the Base for Local Planning with Special Reference to Education, *Manpower Journal*, Vol. XXX, No.1, April-June.

Psacharopoulos, George and Soumelis, Costas (1979). A Quantitative Analysis of the Demand for Higher Education, *Journal of Higher Education.*

Robinson, Joan (1964). *Economic Philosophy*, Pelican Books.

Schultz, T.W. (1962). *Economic Value of Education*, Columbia University Press.

Stone, R. (1954). *The Measurement of Consumer's Expenditure and Behaviour in the United Kingdom*, 1920-1938, Vol. 1, Cambridge University Press.

Stone, R. (1966). "A Model of the Educational System" in Stone, R. (Editor) *Mathematics in the Social Sciences and Other Essays*, Chapman and Hall, London.

10

Education as a Base of Human Development

MANOSI CHAUDHURI, VARIMNA SINGH
and VISHAL AGARWAL

Introduction

In the era of globalization, liberalization and privatization, competitiveness in Indian economy has recorded a significant improvement since 1991, which accelerated the growth of Indian economy. Currently, India is 7th among the 10 fastest growing economies of the world. Among the list of 61 prominent world economies, India was 29th in 2006. To maintain the same pace and momentum, India has to perform exceptionally well in all areas. For growth and for maintaining its momentum, productivity has to play the pivotal role.

The competitive edge depends on the productivity which itself is a function of technology and human capital (Prakash and Balakrishnan, 2006). Accumulation of human capital and its competence and competency, in turn, depends largely upon investment in education and training. Education holds the key to meet the ever rising but changing demand for employment emanating from the dynamic rapid growth of the economy.

In the current mature stage of growth of Indian economy tertiary sector continue to dominate and lead the growth, which is followed by secondary sector. Naturally, employment requirement of tertiary activities are not only more knowledge intensive but their pattern of qualification is also radically different from those of earlier periods. Incidentally, manufacturing has also moved away from mere material processing to information processing which is also highly knowledge intensive.

Such changes as mentioned above have made training for the manpower one of the key objectives of planned development, which requires not only quantitative expansion of education but qualitative improvement and structural change with a bias towards professional and technical education.

Such a human development indicator, as access to education has a strong linkage with the eradication of poverty, and increase in employment and acceleration of growth. The recent enhanced focus on education, is reflected by the allocation for its development in Eleventh Five Year Plan, which shows a visible shift in the approach to growth. The strong focus on education shows a visible shift in the approach to development. However, education was invented as a social sector in the past; it did not receive the desired level of financial support from either the centre or the states. To bridge the gap between the 'haves' and 'have-nots' and to ensure economic growth, access to quality education, specially higher professional education is imperative to produce quality human resource, to reduce social, economic and regional disparities. This is also necessary for generating employment demand of the industries on the one hand, balanced growth and economic development on the other.

Investment in nutrition, hygiene, health, information, knowledge, training and skill formation is needed to transform population into human resource/capital (Prakash, 2000). All these in turn leads to human development.

It is a truism that in this world nothing is constant except change. If the change is autonomous, people of the country lead the change process. If the change is exogenous, then the challenge is great. Since (1) The leaders of the change have to do the ground work for its initiation; and (2) They have to identify and prepare those who have to collaborate and co-operate in nurturing the process of change. This may be directed centrally, or this may also be left to the care of different organizations, including the choice for opting or not opting for change. Thus, irrespective of the source of change it is the human element which has to play the pivotal role (Prakash and Sharma, 2007). The development in the economy since 1991 has produced significant changes in the socio-economic structure of the country and its business and economy. Our per capita income has grown by over 2 per cent a year since 1950. The indicators of quality of life, education, life expectancy, housing, food consumption, etc. have registered significant growth in spite of the fact that our population has more than tripled during the last 60 years. Moreover, while at the time of independence, more than half of our population was living below the poverty line, only about a quarter of our population is now officially classified as poor.

As measured by the social indicators, the performance of the country is less impressive. India ranks low in the Human Development Index. As per the latest Human Development Report of UNDP, India's rank in 2003 was 127 among a total of 177 countries. It is, however, to be noted that India, with the Human Development Index value at 0.6, is included among the Medium Human Development countries. The three components of the Human Development Index are Life Expectancy, Education and per capita GDP. Of these three, India's life expectancy index at 0.64 is near the world average of 0.70. But with respect to education and GDP, our indices at 0.61 and 0.56 are much lower than the world average of 0.77 and 0.75 respectively. Admittedly, the methodology of computation and exclusion of these indices is debatable. Certain facets of human development index may play an important role in the determination of both absolute and relative achievement of a country in the field of human development. For example, there is a continuous process of down/up gradation of qualification of employed manpower in order to cope up with shortage/surplus of available manpower with requisite level and type of education. In case of shortage under qualified persons tend to be employed. In several cases, practical experience and on the job learning is treated as a substitute of formal qualification (for equivalence see T. Lawma, 1992). Rapid growth of professional education has further led to substitution of Journal by professional quantification (for alternative approach to HDI see Prakash, 2005 and Mohanty). The HDI also does not take into account many other aspects of social development as well as institutional dimensions like the freedom enjoyed by people in making political and economic choices. The index may thus understate to some extent India's achievements. However, the deficiency of India in terms of health and education facilities has been documented by several other studies as well. The huge population base, widespread scattering of population and low health and education base in 1951, to a great extent account for such deficiency. If, however we consider the index of progress rather than absolute achievement, India may come out with flying colours. It may also be noted that literacy and enrollment are not sufficiently adequate indicator of development (for example see Prakash *et al.,* Literacy and Development, Project Report, NUEPA). Dropouts and failures dilute the importance of enrollment.

According to a recent study, children in the age group of 6-13 not attending school were estimated at 17.80 per cent. Sixty-seven per cent of deliveries were not done in institutions. Twenty-two per cent of the population did not have access to safe drinking water and 14.4 per cent of children were not fully immunized. Nearly 40 per cent of the population are not living in electrified houses. The number of people living below the poverty line is close to 260 million. While in one sense there has been significant progress in the provision of medical and educational facilities as are reflected in the improvement in life expectancy and literacy rates, we still have a long way to go before we can claim a satisfactory level of performance in these areas. This narration leads us to several questions.

The speed and direction of this change have created an environment of discontinuity. Unarguably, it is people who make things happen. It is thus necessary to have a strategic response for developing our people to face these challenges (Kapoor, 2007). Globalization has generated fierce competition, which places heavy demand on companies for high quality and high effectiveness. High quality of products, including services, high performance and productivity hold the key to success. It is human capital which is the critical resource since it furnishes the core competency for competitiveness.

Growth has many dependent variables. But the improvement in the life of citizens is the indicator of growth. So, improvement in the quality of life will reflect the development of the society as a whole. Globalization has affected the career expectation of individuals and the structure of employment; the skills of the workforce have now become a powerful weapon (Kapoor, 2007).

Education is of great intrinsic importance for their reducing inequalities of opportunity. It is also an important determinant of individual and income, health (and that of their children) and capacity to interact and communicate with others. Inequality in education thus contributes to inequality in other important dimensions of well-being. Measuring inequality in education is not an easy task (World Bank—Equity and Development, World Development Report 2006).

This statement makes the importance of education clear in different aspects of development of an individual. Education is an instrument for developing an economically prosperous society and for ensuring the individual and national development. However, high levels of competence and great degree of competency have become scares because of ever increasing demand for such personnel. The education sector has to catch up with the manpower demand released from the fast growing sectors of Indian economy. Thus education has a crucial role to play, which may even be greater than the role it has played in the second half of the 20th century. This paper attempts to focus on this aspect.

Background/History

India had very strong, sound domestic and internationally acclaimed system of education, including higher education. In ancient India, there was strong '*Guru-shishya*' parampara with highly reputed universities like Takshila in North, Nalanda and Vikramshila in East, Vallabhi in Kathiawad, Kanchi in South and Nadia in Bengal. But, a new era started with the British initiative in 19th century.

In 1882, the first Indian Education Commission, under the chairmanship of W. W. Hunter was constituted. The report dealt with indigenous education, primary education, secondary education and university education. In 1913, the education policy was developed by British government. The Sergent Report of 1944 was an effort to develop a national system of education in India, which suggested the formation of University Grants Commission.

During the post-Independence period, the First Education Commission was constituted in 1948 and it was chaired by Dr. S. Radhakrishnan. The Commission points out "democracy depends for its very life on high standard of general, vocational and professional education. The dissemination of learning, incessant search for new knowledge, unceasing effort to plumb the meaning of life, provision for professional education to satisfy occupational needs of our society are the vital tasks of higher education."

In 1964 and 1968, National Policy on Education was adopted and emphasized the "elimination of disparities, equal access to every Indian of requisite merit, enhancement in support to research and inter-disciplinary research promotion."

Literacy, Education and Development

"Literacy is the ability to identify, understand, interpret, create, communicate and compute, using printed and written materials, associated with the varying contexts. Literacy involves a continuum of learning to enable an individual to achieve his or her goals, to develop his or her knowledge and potential, and to participate fully in the wider society." It facilitates the training and retraining of the employed that is warranted by the change in technology. Though, average completed school years by the workforce shall offer a better index than this (Prakash and Buragohain, 1992).

Education means 'to draw out', facilitating the realization of self-potential and latent talents of individuals. The philosophy of education is the study of the purpose, nature and ideal content of education. Related topics include knowledge itself, the nature of the knowing mind and the human subject, problems of authority, and the relationship between education and society. At least since Locke's time, the philosophy of education has been linked to theories of developmental psychology and human development. Education is perceived as a place where children can develop according to their unique needs and potentialities (Schofield, 1999). The purpose of education can be to develop every individual to their full potential

Fundamental purposes that have been proposed for education include:

- Society depends on educating young people to become responsible, thoughtful and enterprising citizens. This is an intricate, challenging task requiring deep understanding of ethical principles, moral values, political theory, aesthetics, and economics.
- Education is thus a means to foster the individual's, society's, and even humanity's future development and prosperity. Emphasis is often put on economic success in this regard.
- Education can thus attempt to give a firm foundation for the achievement of personal fulfilment.

Education as a critical input in Human Resource Development and in the country's economic growth reiterated the fact that though the major indicator of socio-economic development and growth of the economy, birth rate, death rate, literacy rate, enrolment rate, employment and unemployment are interlinked, the literacy rate is stated to be a major determinant of the rise and fall of the indicators.

It is, however, an extremely crude index (for detail analysis see Prakash *et al.,* 1994).

In 1960s, Shultz as well as Denison (1962) showed that education contributes directly to the growth of national income by improving skills and productive capacities of workforce. The contribution of education to growth will be even stronger, if the complementarities between education and other forms of investment are taken into account (Pasacharopoulos, 1984).

When economies move from lower to higher stages of development, technological base of the economies is also upgraded. This in turn necessitate enhancement of the skills and knowledge of the existing human power. Upgradation of technological base of production raises knowledge and skill requirements of manpower warranted by operationalization of advance technology for production. Thus, manpower planning becomes significant element of educational and economic planning for development. This makes manpower requirements as one of the important approaches to educational planning (Prakash, 1977).

The manpower approach to educational planning, needs determination of different levels and types of education that is essential to attain a certain target growth rate of GNP. GNP is divided into different sectors, having different manpower structure. The need of manpower with different levels and types of education is to be estimated from this structured diversity. But post-manpower forecast prove that the estimates are far away from actual requirements. This is not peculiar to manpower estimates alone.

If we assume education as an investment, then we may look at it as an individual investment and social investment. Under conditions of perfect competition, individual investment would be made if the internal rate of return on investment in education was greater than the market rate of interest. The social investment criterion is that the resources are to be allocated to level and type of education and years of schooling so as to equalise the marginal "social" rate of return on educational investment (Blaug, *et al.,* 1969). This, however, does not take market imperfections and wage/salary downward rigidities due to institutional framework. Besides, projection of past age—education—earning profile into the future projects current into the future (for details see Prakash, 1977).

Mass education was never a priority during the British period. The colonial rule transformed an intermediate literate society into a predominantly illiterate society (see Prakash, 1995). The greatest failure of the Indian educational system relates to the goal of universalisation of elementary education and unable to transfer the enrolments at primary level to secondary and to tertiary level. At secondary level, vocationalisation has not yielded the desired results. Courses introduced in the vocational stream at the higher secondary level are of nominal nature and they do not really help the students to get the jobs.

Sources of Data

We have the series of data since 1950-51 till 2003-04. Series is discreet in nature but the data have been collected from the Census 1961, 1971, 1981, 1991 and 2001 of Primary, Secondary, Tertiary enrolments and of workforce should precede empirics. But, statistics are also collected from Director General of Employment and Training (DGET), fact book of manpower; Statistics were also collected from Ministry of Human Resource Development, Economic Survey 2004-05 and 2006-07.

Method of Analysis

In this paper, we have used description in terms of proportions and regression function to identify the coefficients of growth at various levels of enrolments at primary (I-V), upper primary (VI-VIII) and elementary (I-VIII) of boys, girls and total at all levels respectively.

Analysis

In post-Independence India, overall school enrolment has increased from 19.2 million in 1950-51 to 128.3 million in 2003-04. Among Primary school boys and girls, there is a gap of 8 million (class I-IV). Middle/higher primary school (class VI-VIII) the enrolment has gone up from 3.1 million to 48.7 million with the gap between boys and girls being 6 million and in high school or 11th and 12th classes, enrolment has gone up from 1.5 million in 1950-51 to 35 million in 2003-04, with the gap of 6 million in male and female enrolments.

Table 10.1 depicts the picture.

Table 10.1: Sex-wise Enrolment by Stages, 1999-2000 to 2003-04 Year

(In million)

	Primary (Grades I-V)			*U Primary (Grades VI-VIII)*		
	Boys	*Girls*	*Total*	*Boys*	*Girls*	*Total*
1999-2000*	64.1	49.5	113.6	25.1	17.0	42.1
2000-2001*	64.0	49.8	113.8	25.3	17.5	42.8
2001-2002*	63.6	50.3	113.9	26.1	18.7	44.8
2002-2003*	65.1	57.3	122.4	26.3	20.6	46.9
2003-2004*	68.4	59.9	128.3	27.3	21.4	48.7
2004-2005*	70.12	61.56	131.69	28.71	22.96	51.67
Annual rate of Growth since 1999-2000	1.70%	5.2%	3.2%	2.2%	6.5%	3.9%

* Provisional

Source: SES, MHRD.

From 1999-2000 to 2004-05, enrolments in the elementary education increased substantially, more with then the upper primary stage. Whereas annual increase in enrolment in primary was 3.2 per cent, for upper primary it was 3.9 per cent. Both in primary as well as upper primary stages, proportionate increase in girls' enrolment were higher than those of boys'. In primary classes, whereas the annual growth rate for boys was 1.7 per cent, the same for girls was 5.2 per cent. Similarly, for upper primary, increase in boys' enrolment was at the rate of 2.2 per cent per year, for girls it was 6.5 per cent.

DISE Data for the last three years, viz. 2003-04, 2004-05 and 2005-06 suggest that the annual growth rates for primary and upper primary levels were 4.4 per cent and 12.5 per cent, respectively. These data also suggest that the growth rate in enrolment for girls were higher than that of the boys both at primary as well as at the upper primary levels (For Primary, boys: 4.1 per cent, girls 4.8 per cent. For upper primary, boys 11.7 per cent, girls 13.8 per cent). Thus, there is a significant difference in the growth rates of enrolments based on SES and DISE data. Probably, the trend indicated using DISE data (higher increases at upper primary level) better reflects the field situation.

Enrolment Ratios

Gross Enrolment Ratio (GER), calculated as a ratio of the gross enrolment of children as a proportion of the total children in the

6 year age group, is an indicator to assess the extent of access of children to education. Over the years, it showed an increase. At primary stage, starting with 94.9 in 1999-2000, it improved to 108.56 per cent in 2004-05. For upper primary, the same was 58.8 per cent and 70.5 per cent respectively in the initial and the terminal years under discussion. Gender parity in the GER, both at primary as well as upper primary stages, was an issue. The gap in GER between boys and girls in primary level was 19 per cent points in 1999-2000. This was reduced to 5.8 per cent points in 2004-05. With respect to upper primary level, it improved from 17.5 per cent points to 9 per cent points during the same period. Table 10.2 below shows it.

Table 10.2: Gross Enrolment Ratios at Primary and Upper Primary Levels

Year	*Primary (I-V)*			*Upper Primary (VI-VIII)*			*Elementary (I-VIII)*		
	Boys	*Girls*	*Total*	*Boys*	*Girls*	*Total*	*Boys*	*Girls*	*Total*
1950-51	60.6	24.8	42.6	20.6	4.6	12.7	46.4	17.7	32.1
1960-61	82.6	41.4	62.4	33.2	11.3	22.5	65.2	30.9	48.7
1970-71	95.5	60.5	78.6	46.5	20.8	33.4	75.5	44.4	61.9
1980-81	95.8	64.1	80.5	54.3	28.6	41.9	82.2	52.1	67.5
1990-91	114	85.5	100.1	76.6	47	62.1	100	70.8	86
1991-92	112.8	86.9	100.2	75.1	49.6	61.4	101.2	73.2	87.7
1992-93	95	73.5	84.6	72.5	48.9	67.5	87.7	65.7	77.2
1993-94	90	73.1	81.9	62.1	45.4	54.2	80.2	63.7	72.3
1994-95	96.6	78.2	87.7	68.9	50	60	87.2	68.8	78.4
1995-96	97.1	79.4	88.6	67.8	49.8	59.3	86.9	69.4	78.5
1996-97	97	80.1	88.8	65.8	49.2	58	85.9	69.4	78
1997-98	99.3	82.2	91.1	66.3	49.7	58.5	87.4	70.7	79.4
1998-99 *	100.9	82.9	92.1	65.3	49.1	57.6	87.6	70.6	79.4
1999-2000*	104.1	85.2	94.9	67.2	49.7	58.8	90.1	72	81.3
2000-01*	104.9	85.9	95.7	66.7	49.9	58.6	90.3	72.4	81.6
2001-02*	105.3	86.9	96.3	67.8	52.1	60.2	90.7	73.6	82.4
2002-03*	97.5	93.1	95.4	65.3	56.2	60.9	85.4	79.3	82.5
2003-04*	100.8	95.7	98.3	66.9	57.7	62.5	88	81.5	84.9
2004-05*	111.4	105.5	108.6	74.8	65.8	70.5	97.6	90.6	94.2

*Provisional.

Source: Selected Educational Statistics 2002-2003, Ministry of Human Resource Development. Economic Survey 2004-2005.

The Net Enrolment Ratio (NER), calculated as a ratio of the enrolment of children of the right age group as a proportion of the total children in the relevant age group, is an indicator to assess the extent of access of children of the target age group. This reflects the internal efficiency of the educational system. Excess of gross over net enrolment ratio reflects the internal inefficiency. The difference may be accounted by dropouts, repetition and have stagnation (see Prakash, 1995, Eal Plg). Under ideal circumstances, the GER and NER should be the same—a phenomenon that can be achieved only when all children of the right age group take admission in schools in grade I, there are no repeaters and no case of dropouts; thereby, no child enrolled in any grade would be under-aged or over-aged. A study of the under/over-aged children based on the DISE data of 2003-04 and 2004-05 suggests that in 2003-04, 16 per cent of primary children in the primary classes were in this category; the share of children in the upper primary stage was 23 per cent. This improved in 2004-05 to 14 per cent and 20 per cent respectively in 2004-05.

Results of Regression Analysis

The yearwise students' enrollment pattern has been analyzed using linear regression analysis. In linear regression analysis equation $y = a + bx$, where outcome '*y*' represent "number of students", '*a*' represent "constant value", '*b*' represent the number of changes of student per year and parameter '*x*' represent "single unit of year".

Sixty-two per cent of the total variation in growth rate is explained by the specified regression function thus as high as 38 per cent of total change in GER of boys appears to be beyond the influence of change in time. This residual may be explainable in terms of other or residual factors. The changes in time explain only 0.3 per cent increase in GER per year. This is extremely low, if we consider the low base of the initial period. However, the growth coefficient is highly significant statistically. Since the value of *t* is high as 5.2.

We may hypothesize that the process of closing up has been in operation through the post-Independence period, which should reduce the difference at this level of education between girls and boys.

Girls at primary level show exponential increase in GER at 0.9 per cent per year nearly three times that of boys at primary level, but, it is still not very satisfactory. But, the growth of coefficient is 12.6 per cent, which is considerably high.

The total variation in growth rate is 82 per cent at primary level of both boys and girls, explained by specified regression function. Thus it is as high as 18 per cent of total change in GER appears to be beyond the influence of change in time. This residual may be explainable in terms of other or residual factors. The changes in time explain only 0.5 per cent increase in GER per year. This is low, if we consider the low base of the initial period. However, the growth coefficient is highly significant statistically, since the value of it is high as 8.9

At upper primary 83 per cent of the total variation in growth rate is explained by specified regression function. Thus it is as high as 17 per cent of total change in GER of boys appears to be beyond the influence of change in time. This residual may be explainable in terms of other or residual factors. The changes in time explain only 0.9 per cent increase in GER per year which is better than that of primary. but still show low transformation of enroll candidates to upper primary levels. However, the growth coefficient is highly significant statistically, since the value of it is high as 9.2.

At upper primary, girls' education shows the total variation in growth rate of 93 per cent, which can be explained by specified regression function. Thus it is as high as 7 per cent of total change in GER of girls which appears to be beyond the influence of change in time. This residual may be explainable in terms of other or residual factors. The changes in time explain only 1.8 per cent increase in GER per year. This is considerably better than that of primary levels girls who have shown better conversion of primary enrolment to upper primary levels However, the growth coefficient is highly significant statistically. Since the value of it is high as 15.8.

At upper primary, the total variation in growth rate is 90 per cent, which is improved than that of primary, explained by specified regression function, as high as 10 per cent of total change in GER of total enrolment at upper primary (VI-VIII) appears to be beyond the influence of change in time. This residual may be explainable in terms of other or residual factors. The changes in time explain only 1.1 per cent increase in GER per year. However, the growth coefficient is highly significant statistically, since the value of it is high as 12.4.

But GER at elementary level (I-VIII) of boys shown the total variation in growth rate of 73 per cent, which can be explained by specified regression function. Thus it is as high as 27 per cent of total change in GER of boys appears to be beyond the influence of change in time. This residual may be explainable in terms of other or residual factors. The changes in time explain only 0.4 per cent increase in GER per year. This is low and the growth coefficient is highly significant statistically, since the value of it is high as 6.8.

But GER at elementary level (I-VIII) of girls shown the total variation in growth rate of 93 per cent, which can be explained by specified regression function, as high as 7 per cent of total change in GER of girls appears to be beyond the influence of change in time. This residual may be explainable in terms of other or residual factors. The changes in time explain only 1.08 per cent increase in GER per year. This is low and the growth coefficient is highly significant statistically, since the value of it is high as 15.44.

The total variation in growth rate of 86 per cent, which can be explained by specified regression function. Thus it is as high as 14 per cent of total change in GER appears to be beyond the influence of change in time. This residual may be explainable in terms of other or residual factors. The changes in time explain only 0.6 per cent increase in GER per year. This is low and the growth coefficient is highly significant statistically, since the value of it is high as 10.56.

Regression Tables

Primary (I-V)	***Boys***			
Regression Statistics				
Multiple R	0.788			
R Square	0.621			
Adjusted R Square	0.5987			
Standard Error	0.038			
Observations	19			
ANOVA				
	df	*SS*	*MS*	*F*
Regression	1	0.0402	0.0402	27.86
Residual	17	0.0245	0.0014	
Total	18	0.0647		
	Coefficients	*Standard Error*	*t Stat*	*P-value*
Intercept	1.8569	0.0262	70.807	2E-22
X Variable 1	0.0032	0.0006	5.2778	6E-05

Primary (I-V)	***Girls***
Regression Statistics	
Multiple R	0.951
R Square	0.9043
Adjusted R Square	0.8987
Standard Error	0.046
Observations	19

(*Contd.*)

(Contd.)

ANOVA				
	df	*SS*	*MS*	*F*
Regression	1	0.3396	0.34	160.653
Residual	17	0.0359	0.002	
Total	18	0.3756		
	Coefficients	*Standard Error*	*t Stat*	*P-value*
Intercept	1.4893	0.0318	46.9	2E-19
X Variable 1	0.0092	0.0007	12.67	4.3E-10
Primary	***Total***			
Regression Statistics				
Multiple R	0.9079			
R Square	0.8242			
Adjusted R Square	0.8139			
Standard Error	0.0391			
Observations	19			
ANOVA				
	df	*SS*	*MS*	*F*
Regression	1	0.12204	0.122	79.71
Residual	17	0.02603	0.0015	
Total	18	0.14807		
	Coefficients	*Standard Error*	*t Stat*	*P-value*
Intercept	1.7083	0.02702	63.223	1E-21
X Variable 1	0.0055	0.00062	8.9282	8E-08
Upper Primary	***Boys***			
Regression Statistics				
Multiple R	0.91327			
R Square	0.83406			
Adjusted R Square	0.8243			
Standard Error	0.05885			
Observations	19			
ANOVA				
	df	*SS*	*MS*	*F*
Regression	1	0.29596	0.296	85.448
Residual	17	0.05888	0.003	
Total	18	0.35485		
	Coefficients	*Standard Error*	*t Stat*	*P-value*
Intercept	1.42312	0.04064	35.02	3E-17
X Variable 1	0.00859	0.00093	9.244	5E-08

(Contd.)

(*Contd.*)

Upper Primary	***Girls***			
Regression Statistics				
Multiple R	0.9677			
R Square	0.9365			
Adjusted R Square	0.9328			
Standard Error	0.0742			
Observations	19			
ANOVA				
	df	*SS*	*MS*	*F*
Regression	1	1.3795	1.3795	250.8
Residual	17	0.0935	0.0055	
Total	18	1.473		
	Coefficients	*Standard Error*	*t Stat*	*P-value*
Intercept	0.8203	0.0512	16.018	1E-11
X Variable 1	0.0185	0.0012	15.837	1E-11

Upper Primary	***Total***			
Regression Statistics				
Multiple R	0.94905			
R Square	0.90069			
Adjusted R Square	0.89485			
Standard Error	0.06045			
Observations	19			
ANOVA				
	Df	*SS*	*MS*	*F*
Regression	1	0.56338	0.56338	154.186
Residual	17	0.06212	0.00365	
Total	18	0.6255		
	Coefficients	*Standard Error*	*t Stat*	*P-value*
Intercept	1.21294	0.04174	29.0584	6.2E-16
X Variable 1	0.01185	0.00095	12.4172	6E-10

Elementary	***Boys***
Regression Statistics	
Multiple R	0.855
R Square	0.732
Adjusted R Square	0.716
Standard Error	0.04
Observations	19

(*Contd.*)

(*Contd.*)

ANOVA				
	df	SS	MS	F
Regression	1	0.07518	0.07518	46.3482
Residual	17	0.02757	0.00162	
Total	18	0.10275		
	Coefficients	*Standard Error*	*t Stat*	*P-value*
Intercept	1.745	0.02781	62.7623	1.5E-21
X Variable 1	0.004	0.00064	6.80795	3E-06
Elementary	***Girls***			
Regression Statistics				
Multiple R	0.96617			
R Square	0.93348			
Adjusted R Square	0.92957			
Standard Error	0.04441			
Observations	19			
ANOVA				
	Df	*SS*	*MS*	*F*
Regression	1	0.47049	0.47049	238.57
Residual	17	0.03353	0.00197	
Total	18	0.50401		
	Coefficients	*Standard Error*	*t Stat*	*P-value*
Intercept	1.34317	0.03067	43.8001	6E-19
X Variable 1	0.01083	0.0007	15.4457	2E-11
Elementary	***Total***			
Regression Statistics				
Multiple R	0.93159			
R Square	0.86786			
Adjusted R Square	0.86008			
Standard Error	0.04025			
Observations	19			
ANOVA				
	df	*SS*	*MS*	*F*
Regression	1	0.18084	0.1808	111.648
Residual	17	0.02753	0.0016	
Total	18	0.20837		
	Coefficients	*Standard Error*	*t Stat*	*P-value*
Intercept	1.59026	0.02779	57.222	7E-21
Xz Variable 1	0.00671	0.00064	10.566	6.9E-09

Conclusion

The main findings of the study are to focus on development of population depending largely on education. The analysis reflects the serious gaps between different classes or groups of the society, different regions of the country, which is quite alarming. The issues which need attention are illiteracy rate, dropout rate in the schools (Pre-primary, primary, secondary, and tertiary) and their possible remedies. The number is very limited which is contributing to the national economy and human resource development. We consider this is a joint responsibility of all stakeholders, which needs coordinated efforts and definite commitment to improve the system.

There are several positive sides in India's educational development. Its primary school enrolment has come close to being universal and current attendance rates as well as literacy rates have risen encouragingly in recent times. However, Indian achievements in other respects leave much to be desired. Firstly, secondary school participation is still low and unequally distributed. Since economic incentives for acquiring secondary schooling are very high, demand for secondary schooling is likely to be strong suggesting that greater participation is hindered by a combination of constrained supply of secondary schools and household credit-constraints. Secondly, learning achievements in both primary and secondary schooling are very low, signaling poor quality schooling. Thirdly, and relatedly, school facilities/inputs are low and teacher absenteeism is high.

REFERENCES

Blaug, M., Layard, P.R.G. and Woodhall, M. (1969): *Causes of Graduate Unemployment in India*, Allen Lane, London.

DISE (2006): Elementary Education in India: Analytical Report 2005, District Information System for Education, NIEPA, New Delhi.

Dongaonkar, Dayanand, (2004): Issues in Higher Education, In *Issues in Higher Education*, Vol. 2 Ed by Venkata Subramanian, Hyderabad, ICFAI Press.

Educational Statistics (2002-03). Ministry of Human Resource Development.

Kapoor, B.M, (2007): HRD Development Today, *Challenges and Strategies,* p. 9, Vol. 33.

Kingdon, G. (1994). An Economic Evaluation of School Management-types in India: A Case Study of Uttar Pradesh, Unpublished D. Phil. thesis, Economics Department, Oxford University.

Lawma, T. (1992): *Market Imperfections and Manpower Planning*, Common Wealth Publications, Delhi.

Mehta, Arun C. (2005): *Elementary Education in India*, State Report Cards, NIEPA, New Delhi.

Prakash, S. (1996): *Cost of Education*, Anamika, Delhi.

Prakash, S. (1999): *Educational Planning*, Gyan Publishing House, New Delhi.

Prakash, S. (2000): Utilization of Human Resources Concept and Empirical Illustrations, *Business Perspective*, Vol. 2, No. 2, July-December.

Prakash, S. and Balakrishnan, Brinda (2006). Managerial Approach to Conceptualization of Development and Growth Convergence of Macro to Micro Theory, *Business Perspective*, Vol. 8, No. 2, July-December.

Prakash, S. and Buragohain, T. (1993): Indicators of Educational Development: Analysis of Average completed School Years in India, *Journal of Educational Planning and Administration*, Vol. 7, No 1.

Prakash, S. (1977): *Educational System—An Econometric Study*, Concept, New Delhi.

Prakash, S., Gupta, Abha and Buragohain, T. (1990): Economic Growth and Literacy: International Experience, *Journal of Educational Planning and Administration*, Vol. 3, Nos. 1-2, Special Issue on Educational Planning and Management in the Third World.

Psacharopoulos, G. and Woodhall, M. (1985): *Education for Development—An Analysis of Investment Choices*, Oxford University Press.

Schultz, T.W. (1960): Capital Formation by Education, *Journal of Political Economy*.

Schultz, T.W. (1963): *Economic Value of Education*, Colombia University Press.

Sharma, Amit, (2007): Educational Development and Human resource Qualifications in Indian Job market, *Business Perspective*, Vol. 9, No. 1. January-June.

UNDP, (2005): Human Development Report, Oxford, Oxford University Press.

UNESCO, (2006): *Higher Education in the World*: Statistical Overview, Paris, UNESCO.

University Grants Commission, Annual Report.

World Bank (2006): Secondary Education in India: Investing in the future. Human Development Unit, South Asia Region, World Bank, draft, April 2006.

World Bank, (2006): *Equity and Development: World Bank Report*, New York, Oxford University Press.

11

Human Resource Development under Competitive Regime: Context-India; Perspective-Asia

ARUP BARMAN

Introduction

Human development is primarily, about allowing people to lead a life that they value and 'enabling them to realize their potential as human beings. The normative framework for human development is today reflected in the broad vision set out in the Millennium Development Goals, the internationally agreed set of time bound goals for reducing extreme poverty, extending gender equality and advancing opportunities for health and education. Progress towards these objectives provides a benchmark for assessing the international community's resolve in translating commitments into action[1]. More than that, it is a condition for building shared prosperity and collective security in our increasingly interdependent world. There is now less than 8 years to go to the 2015 target date for achieving the Millennium Development Goals—the time-bound targets of the international community for reducing extreme poverty and hunger, cutting child deaths, getting children good education and overcoming gender inequalities. Still, we sometimes face the question about the need for human development at both micro and macro levels from some so-called intellectuals in our society. *They argue in favour of resource-based concept, cite the examples of developed countries and their possession of resources and the critical mass. This group propagates that the development is an outcome of only resources possessed by the developed nation other than human resources. For availability of resources the critical intellectuals migrate to a resource full geographical region or nation, later on, they dominate the surroundings by combining non-human resources and through their intellectual prowess commercially, either socially, or politically.* The present paper does not like to argue against the pitiable logic of so-called intellectuals who support 'the resources other than human resources are the key for development of a nation' or 'an inhuman logic of for development'. Human Development is a globally accepted issue, 177 countries of the world is giving attention to this issue and it is being monitored by the United Nations Development Programme. After liberalization, almost all nations of the world understood the need for human development. There are myriad number of researches serving as the strong evidences on linkages of Human Development and Economic Development. Naturally, all the developed countries are well equipped with a high level of human development and as a result, they are far more advanced in almost all fronts of competition. After liberalization, almost all the countries of the world have embraced competition. In this competition, a few Asian tigers are showing their competence in the developmental arena that may be considered as Rapid Developing Countries (RDCs). These RDCs are—Singapore, Thailand, Hong Kong, and Korea. At the same time, most of the countries of Asia whether developing or underdeveloped, are trying to follow the overall Asian growth trajectory under the competitive regime. India as a developing country is also well known for its human resources and the competitive drive undertaken after the liberalization. Under the competitive regime how Indian subcontinent is performing its role for translating the commitment into action, needs a fresh look.

Objectives of the Study

The basic aim of the study is to highlight the present state of India's Human Development in contrast to state of competition and economic transition of Asia.

To achieve the above aim the present paper would proceed to achieve the following objectives—

1. To draw a picture of India's human development performance in contrast to the countries of different regions of Asia;

Table 11:1 Human Development Trend, Human Development Index (Score)

Groups	1975	1980	1985	1990	1995	2000	2004	Annual growth Rate (1975-2004)	Annual Growth Rate (1990-2004)
East Asia									
China (PR)	0.527	0.560	0.569	0.628	0.685	0.785	0.768	0.13	0.15
Hong Kong	0.761	0.801	0.829	0.864	0.863	0.917	0.927	0.18	0.19
Korea ®	0.712	0.746	0.786	0.923	0.863	0.890	0.912	0.17	0.19
Mongolia	—	—	0.642	0.646	0.634	0.669	0.691	0.13	0.14
South East Asia									
Cambodia	—	—	—	—	0.536	0.545	0.583	0.12	0.09
Indonesia	0.469	0.532	0.585	0.626	0.665	0.682	0.711	0.13	0.14
Lao PDR	—	—	0.425	0.451	0.488	0.523	0.553	0.10	0.11
Malaysia	0.616	0.659	0.696	0.723	0.761	0.791	0.805	0.15	0.16
Philippines	0.655	0.689	0.695	0.722	0.738	0.759	0.763	0.15	0.16
Singapore	0.727	0.763	0.786	0.823	0.862	—	0.916	0.14	0.14
Thailand	0.615	0.664	0.680	0.717	0.751	0.775	0.784	0.15	0.16
Vietnam	—	—	—	0.618	0.661	0.696	0.709	0.14	0.14
South Asia									
Bangladesh	0.347	0.366	0.391	0.422	0.454	0.510	0.530	0.09	0.10
India	o.413	0.439	0.477	0.515	0.548	0.577	0.611	0.11	0.12
Maldives	—	—	—	—	—	—	—		
Pakistan	0.365	0.383	0.420	0.463	0.449	0.511	0.539	0.09	0.10
Sri Lanka	0.612	0.653	0.684	0.706	0.729	0.747	0.755	0.14	0.15
Mean	*0.5824*	*0.605*	*0.619*	*0.657*	*0.668*	*0.692*	*0.722*	*0.13*	*0.14*
Std. Dev	*0.140*	*0.148*	*0.146*	*0.150*	*0.141*	*0.134*	*0.133*		

Source: Human Development Report, 2006.

2. To examine the direction of India's human development in the light of competition and economic transition and competition in Asia; and
3. An attempt has been made for initiation of HRD efforts for sustainable human development for India to fit the future direction of competition in Asia.

Methodology

The study is conducted with a mix of empirical and desk research method, attempts to draw inferences from secondary sources of data and attempts to triangulate through the blending of views of multi-angled literatures and data analysis as felt fit to the objectives of the paper.

Linkages to Human Development and Poverty

The linkage between human development and economic performance is critical. However, it would be quite logical to bring forth the context of linkages of economic performance with human development. If the logic of human being as the end for the efforts for human development is an accepted logic then the economic performance of a country should reduce the gap of poverty of a country. To substantiate, human development (ranks) and poverty ranks for year 2004 (from the Human Development Report, Index-2006) were taken into account for further analysis (Table 11.2). Table 11.2 indicates the relationship between lower rank of human development and higher ranks for poverty for the referred countries. To test and to objectively substantiate the linkage between the poverty with the human development of the countries of Asian Sub-Region a test was conducted by applying the statistical tools, namely—Kendal tau-c, Kendal tau-b, Gamma (γ) Test, Spearman Correlation, and Pearson's Correlation incorporated in the Cross Tab of SPSS. The result of analysis revealed Kendal Tau-b a non-parametric measure of association for ordinal or ranked variables that consider ties. The sign of the coefficient indicates the positive direction of the relationship, and its absolute value = 0.886 indicates the strength, with larger absolute values indicating stronger relationships. Kendal tau-c also non-parametric measure of association for ordinal variables ignores ties. The sign of the coefficient = 0.886 also indicates the

Symmetric Measures

	Tests	*Value*	*Asymp. Std. Error*	*Approx. T*	*Approx. Sig.*
Ordinal by Ordinal	Kendall's tau-b	0.886	0.072	12.254	0.000
	Kendall's tau-c	0.886	0.072	12.254	0.000
	γ (gamma)	0.886	0.072	12.254	0.000
	Spearman Correlation	0.964	0.033	13.127	0.000
Interval by Interval	Pearson's R	0.914	0.023	8.128	0.000

Table 11.2: HDI and Global Competitiveness

Groups	*HDI Rank (Global-177 Country)*	*Global Competitiveness (Rank)*
East Asia		
China	81	NA
Hong Kong	22	11
Korea (Rep)	NA	25
Mongolia	116	92
Taipei (China)	NA	NA
South East Asia		
Cambodia	129	103
Indonesia	108	50
Lao PDR	133	
Malaysia	61	26
Philippines	84	71
Singapore	25	5
Thailand	74	35
Vietnam	109	NA
South Asia		
Bangladesh	137	99
India	126	43
Maldives	98	
Sri Lanka	93	79
Pakistan	134	91

Source: Human Development Report, 2006.

direction of the positive relationship, and its absolute value indicates the strength, with larger absolute values indicating stronger relationships. Gamma (zero-order for 2-way tables and conditional for 3-way to 10-way tables), Kendall's tau-b, and Kendall's tau-c. Commonly used non-parametric measure of correlation (coefficient = 0.886) between two ordinal variables. For all of the cases, the values of each of the variables were ranked from smallest to largest, and the Pearson correlation coefficient is computed on the ranks of which coefficient = 0.964. For tables in which both rows and columns contain ordered values, Correlations yields Spearman's correlation coefficient, (ρ) rho (numeric data only). Spearman's (ρ) rho is a measure of association between rank orders (coefficient = 0.914). All coefficients were statistically significant at 0.0001 (P = 0.000<0.0001) by accepting 33 per cent and 23 per cent error Spearman's rho, and Pearson's Coefficient of correlation revealed very strong correlation. However, the numbers of country were only 14 in the present study, sample was small, obvious reason for higher order of standard error. Since the value of coefficients are very high with very high order of significance, henceforth, the findings may be useful for hypothesizing the relationship between the poverty and human development ranks. Finally, a hypothesis was framed, i.e. H = Country having higher rank for human development shows lower rank in human poverty, and lower the human development rank shows higher ranks in human poverty. The hypothetical relation indicates the logic of lower the human development of country with higher poverty and *vice versa*. Provided the poverty indicators are taken from the UNDP definitions and analysis of HDI.

Highlight on Economic Transition in Asia

Most economies in developing Asia and the Pacific present two main differences between today and three decades ago. The first relates to size: they have grown significantly. The second relates to their look and form: they have changed. Countries become different as they grow, in terms of not only what they produce, but also how they produce and the ways in which they change matter for growth. In Asian context, growth occurs through diversification and the birth and expansion of new economic activities and assimilation of better methods of organization and production. They followed a path of population migration from countryside to town, and resources moved out of agriculture and into industry and services: they changed. The celebrated "logistic model of growth" (Kuznets, 1966, 1971; Chenery, 1977) captures these features but suggests that *transformation is almost automatic*—ingrained in technological progress and in the *way needs and tastes change with rising incomes*. Developing Asia's experience certainly confirms that change is deeply ingrained in growth and that change has been evolutionary rather revolutionary.

Countries that have grown have changed their form continuously, not by great leaps and countries that have struggled tend to display structural inertia. Reversals have also occurred. The newly industrialized countries of developing Asia (NIEs) are approaching completion of the catch-up process, i.e., they are reaching rich-country, per capita income levels. On their past trends, their productivity levels and incomes will soon converge on levels seen in the countries of the Organization for Economic Co-operation and Development (OECD). The NIEs are now facing the challenges of bringing of economic maturity. Other countries, like Malaysia and Thailand, are closing the gap, but still have to navigate more changes if they are to sustain progress. In the People's Republic of China (PRC) and India, as well as in other countries like Cambodia and Pakistan, the pace of change is quickening and incomes are rising, but many potential challenges still lie ahead. The young countries of Central Asia also face enormous challenges, though their natural resource industries present opportunities, provided rents are invested sensibly. However, for small countries that are also often handicapped by geography, options are more limited. They will have to incubate their own models of economic growth and change, drawing largely on local resources and capabilities.

The growth dynamics of different countries reinforces one another, and a conspicuous process of integration of production, trade and investment takes place. National development processes and transformations are going on in a regional context and create a regional dynamics, regional transformation, and due to restructuring of the global production networks, *Asian development models* and their societal and institutional underpinnings are in the process of changing. The regional dynamic in Asia contributes to the creation of new kinds of production networks and commodity chains; new regional and global business networks are emerging, and increasingly trans-Pacific transports links are surpassing the old core routes of world trade in the Atlantic. India is also undergoing a strong process of economic transformation. The Indian breakthrough in software has spread to other sectors. India's economic relations with East and Southeast Asia are still quite limited, but it may in the future choose to integrate in the emerging regional economic network in Asia. In short, a complex pattern of *Asian and global 'networks'* is emerging. During four decades, the so-called High-Performing Asian Economies in East and Southeast Asia have outperformed most other developing regions.Though they in many ways represent different 'varieties of capitalism' (models), they also have many similarities (the East Asian Model). They have all become exporters of manufactured goods and have followed the same development trajectory from light industries to heavy industries and further to knowledge intensive manufacturing and service production.

Developing Asia needs to grow and create wealth to tackle poverty and other forms of human deprivation. However, at the same time, developing Asia must create jobs for those who are at present unemployed and underemployed—on some estimates as many as 425 million workers. New workers who are about to enter the labour force will also need decent jobs. In most countries, the profile of economic activity has moved from agriculture to industry and services. However, there seems to be much greater complexity about the way in which patterns of industrial diversification and specialization evolve that may be linked to the sustainability of growth. Major challenges lie in developing Asia in *Walking on two legs* that considers possible broad strategies for future growth and job creation. For most countries, both industrial and services development are likely to have an important role to play. In the context of the countries of Asia too, complementarities between industry and services can be understood, as is the role of services as a provider of jobs.

Indian Competitiveness in Contrast to Asian Sub-Regions

The scenario of global competitiveness can be well understood from the Global Competitive Report (Table 11.3). For comparing India's Global Competitiveness in contrast to economy of different sub-regions of Asia, score on the different indicators are taken into consideration. The scores were taken from the Report-2007. Let us first observe India's competitiveness in contrast to East Asian Highly Competitive Economy. In Table 11.4 the first slot is devoted for comparison of East Asian economy, and Fig. 11.1 showing India's competitiveness in contrast to east Asia. The figure revealed India's institution competitiveness score is lower than Hong Kong; infrastructural competence is lower than that of China and Hong Kong; macro economy competence is lower than China, Hong Kong, Korea. For the indicator Health and Primary Education Indian competitiveness is equal to China and Hong Kong but less than Korea.

Table 11.3: Global Competitiveness of Asian Sub-Regions

	Global Compt. (Rank)	Institutions	Infrastructure	Macro-economy	Health and Primary Education	Higher Education and Training	Market Efficiencies	Technological Readiness	Business Sophistication	Innovation	Overall Com. Index
East Asia											
China (PR)	54	3.51	3.54	5.72	6.44	3.68	4.22	3.07	4.05	3.44	4.26
Hong Kong	11	5.54	6.29	5.65	6.67	5.08	5.69	5.44	5.48	4.46	5.46
Korea ®	24	4.18	5.38	5.48	6.85	5.38	4.39	5.22	5.20	4.71	5.13
Mongolia	92	3.31	2.24	4.46	5.82	3.89	3.62	2.60	2.98	2.86	3.60
South East Asia											
Cambodia	50	3.26	2.72	4.52	6.35	4.25	4.43	3.17	4.53	3.60	3.39
Indonesia	103	4.04	2.72	4.52	6.35	4.25	4.43	3.17	4.53	3.60	4.26
Lao PDR											
Malaysia	24	5.12	5.09	4.97	6.58	4.80	5.24	4.64	5.29	4.53	5.44
Philippines	71	3.38	2.73	4.45	6.20	4.02	4.21	3.32	4.20	3.05	4.00
Singapore	5	5.90	6.16	5.67	6.81	5.59	5.62	5.69	5.17	5.04	5.63
Thailand	35	4.34	4.36	5.10	6.09	4.44	4.76	3.64	4.57	3.74	4.58
Vietnam		3.62	2.79	4.63	6.43	3.39	4.10	2.85	3.55	3.10	–
South Asia											
Bangladesh	99	2.88	2.03	4.72	6.04	2.68	3.93	2.41	3.42	2.59	3.46
India	43	4.45	3.50	4.12	5.90	4.35	5.07	3.52	5.06	4.14	4.44
Pakistan	91	3.51	3.36	4.19	4.79	2.82	4.23	2.77	4.05	3.27	3.66
Sri Lanka	79	3.48	3.07	3.66	6.66	3.56	4.10	2.87	3.90	3.32	3.87

In the direction of higher education and training Indian competitiveness is equivalent to Hong Kong, but lower than the score of Korea; India's technological readiness is less than Korea and Hong Kong. India is a high performer in business sophistication as equal to Hong Kong, but higher than China and Korea.

In contrast to competitiveness of South East Asia, Indian competitiveness do not reveal a wide gap. Obviously overall competitiveness of India in contrast to Malaysia and Singapore reveals a great contrast (Fig. 11.2), because overall rank of Malaysia and Singapore is far above than India's competitiveness. Indian institutional competitiveness in contrast to Malaysia and Singapore is lower and India's infrastructural competitiveness is lower than that of Singapore and Malaysia. India's competitiveness in macro economic front is far below that of Malaysia and Singapore. Health and Primary Education of both Singapore and Malaysia is

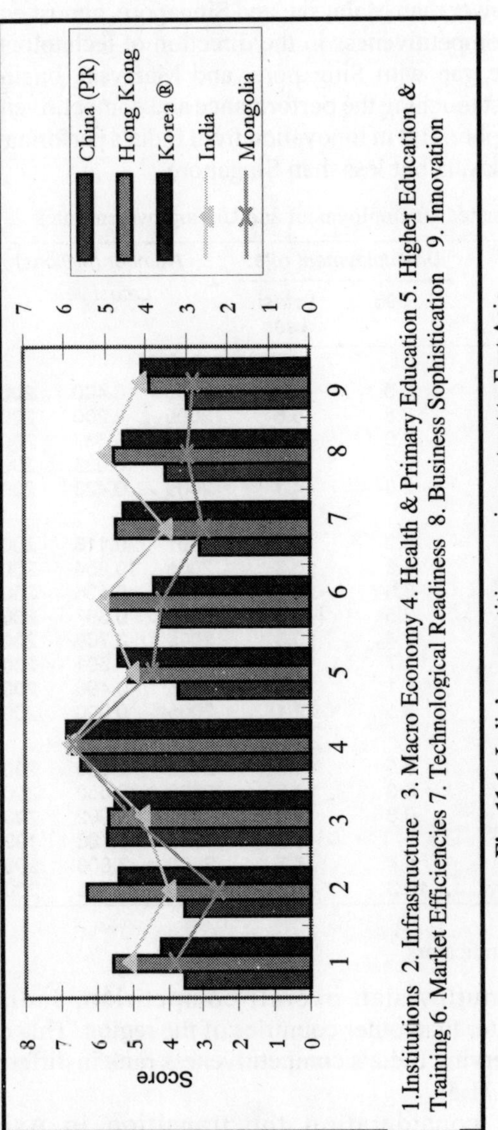

1.Institutions 2. Infrastructure 3. Macro Economy 4. Health & Primary Education 5. Higher Education & Training 6. Market Efficiencies 7. Technological Readiness 8. Business Sophistication 9. Innovation

Fig. 11.1: India's competitiveness in contrast to East Asia

quite higher than India; India's higher education and training are lower than that of Malaysia and Singapore, but almost equal to Thailand. Market efficiency is lower than Malaysia, and Singapore, almost equal to Thailand. India's competitiveness in the direction of technological readiness shows wide gap with Singapore, and Malaysia, business sophistication is almost touching the performance and competitiveness of Malaysia and Singapore. But in Innovation front India's performance is almost equal to Malaysia but less than Singapore.

Table 11.4 : Estimated Unemployment and Unemployment rates

Country	Unemployment rates			Number (Millions)	
	1996	Latest year		Latest year	
East Asia					
China, People's Rep. of	3.0	4.2	2005	8.400	2005
Hong Kong, China	2.8	5.6	2005	0.200	2000
Korea, Rep. of	2.0	3.7	2005	0.887	2005
Mongolia	6.7	3.3	2005	0.033	2005
Taipei, China	2.6	4.1	2005	0.428	2005
Southeast Asia					
Cambodia	0.9	1.8	2001	0.116	2001
Indonesia	4.9	10.3	2005	10.854	2005
Lao People's Dem. Rep.[a]	3.6	5.1	2003	0.136	2003
Malaysia	2.5	3.5	2005	0.367	2005
Philippines	7.4	10.3	2005	3.766	2005
Singapore	1.7	3.1	2005	.301	2005
Thailand	1.1	1.4	2005	0.496	2005
Viet Nam[b]	3.5	2.1	2005	0.900	2005
South Asia					
Bangladesh	3.5	4.3	2003	2.000	2003
India[c]	6.0	7.3	2000	9.050	2000
Maldives[a]	0.8	2.0	2001	0.002	2001
Nepal		1.8	1999	0.180	1999
Pakistan	5.4	7.7	2005	3.600	2005
Sri Lanka	11.3	7.7	2005	0.623	2005

a 1995. b 1998. c 1994.
Source: 2006 ADB Key Indicators.

Compared to South Asian overall competition, India's performance is far better than other countries of the region. This can be understood by observing India's competitiveness rank in different directions as in Table 11.5.

By taking into consideration the transition in Asian competitiveness, we can find a few observable challenges. These are—(a) First, developing Asia needs to grow and create wealth to tackle poverty and other forms of human deprivation. However, at

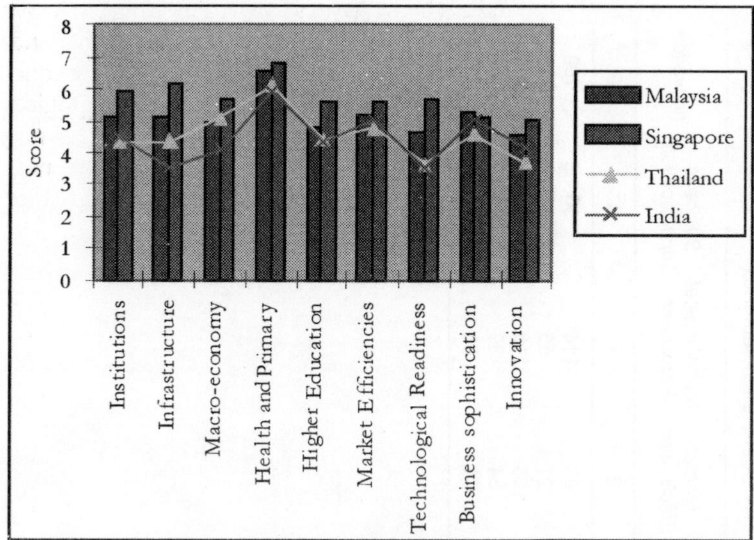

Fig. 11.2: India's Conpetitiveness in Contrast to South East Asian Highly Competitive Economy

the same time, developing Asia must create jobs for those who are at present unemployed and underemployed, (b) Secondly, Asian economies are facing the threshold of competition. Numerous studies concluded that the trend of competition in Asian economy is human based, where human development plays a critical role. Responding to Globe and Asian transition and competitiveness India also converged to direction as needed by time and situation. India could adopt service and knowledge economy and enter the global competition since libralization. India's potential in the global competitiveness stood as 43rd Rank among 125 competitive countries. In the light of these facts it is necessary to appreciate the state of human development in contrast to nations of Asian Sub-Regions to understand status of human development.

Trend of Indian HD in Contrast to Asian Sub-Region

To describe objectively on the state of human development in India the present section of the paper has taken the help of overall score of human development indicators as appeared in the reports since 1975 to 2006. The available composite score comparison in the

Table 11.5: Global Competitiveness Ranking of Five South Asian countries

Pillar Sector	Institutions	Infrastructure	Macro-economy	Health and Primary Education	Higher Education and Training	Market Efficiencies	Technological Readiness	Business Sophistication	Innovation
	1	2	3	4	5	6	7	8	9
Bangladesh	121	117	47	90	108	83	114	96	109
India	34`	60	88	93	49	21	55	25	26
Nepal	99	122	59	102	109	105	116	108	112
Pakistan	79	67	86	108	104	54	89	66	60
Sri Lanka	82	76	110	36	81	71	83	71	53

Source: ADO, Asian Development Bank.

Human Development Report-2006 for world suggests deriving the developmental trend by taking data with a gap for five years for countries of regional block of Asia. India's human development trend is drawn in contrast to the trends of development of the countries of each region of Asia. The yearwise scores for each country and countries of the regional block of Asia appeared in Table 11.1 (of Appendix). As time passes, human development of each country (Table 11.1) revealed upward and rising trend. By comparing India's trend with trends of countries of East-Asia, i.e. with Hong Kong, China, Korea we can find the contrast for HD in East Asia. The score difference between China and India were (0.527-0.413) = 0.114 for year 1975; (0.560-0.439) = 0.121 for year 1980; (0.566-0.477) = 0.099 for the year 1985; (0.628-0.515) = 0.113 for the year 1990; (0.685-0.545) = 0.140 for the year 1995; (0.785-0.577) = 0.208 for the year 2000; (0.768-0.611) = 0.157 for the latest year 2004 of the HD Report, 2006. The score differences between China and India are revealing increasing level of gap of HD between two countries.

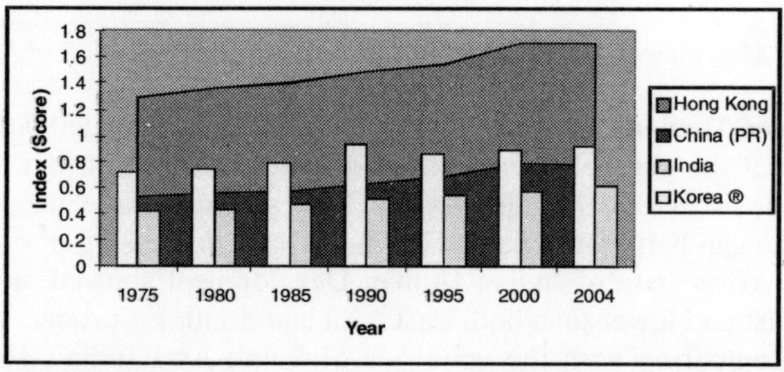

Note: Comparison to East Asian countries Indian HD performance was very low.

Fig. 11.3: Human Development (India and East Asia)

In contrast to the countries of South East Asia (Philippines, Malaysia, Lao PDR, Thailand, Singapore) India's human development performance was very low during the period 1975-2004. India's performance in context of HD was below the lowest performer of South East Asian blocks, i.e. Thailand (Fig.11.4; Table 11.1 of Appendix). Comparing the score of India and Thailand, we can derive the gap of human development between the lowest ranked performers of South East Asia and India. The score difference between Thailand

and India were (0.615-0.413) = 0.202 for year 1975; (0.664-0.439) = 0.225 for year 1980; (0.680-0.477) = 0.213 for the year 1985; (0.717-0.515) = 0.202 for the year 1990; (0.751-0.545) = 0.214 for the year 1995; (0.775-0.577) = 0.198 for the year 2000; (0.784-0.611) = 0.173 for the latest year 2004 of the HD Report, 2006. The score gaps

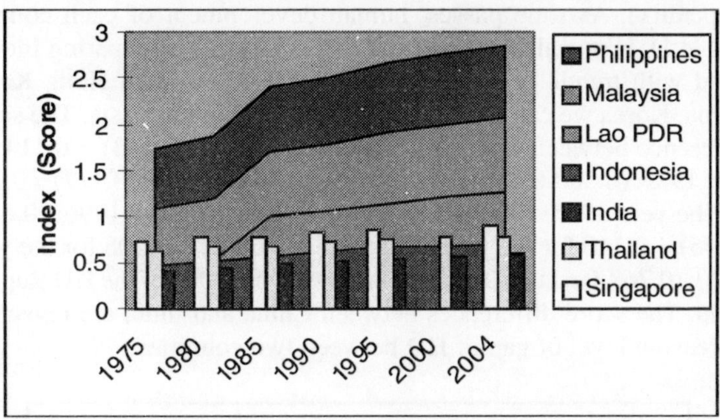

Fig. 11.4: Human Development Performance (India and South East Asia)

between Thailand and India for period of 30 years revealed opposite trend of the gap between China and India. During last part of the period, 1975-2004 the gap between China and India were increasing, but the gap between India and Thailand were decreasing. From this comparison state of Indian Human Development showed, a sharp contrast and lower than both East Asia and South East Asia.

Comparing with the countries of South Asia India's Human Development performance was 2nd in position next to Sri Lanka. The wide score gaps exist between India and Sri Lankan human development (Figure 11.5; Table 11.1 of Appendix).

The score difference between Sri Lanka and India were (0.612-0.413) = 0.199 for year 1975; (0.653-0.439) = 0.214 for year 1980; (0.684-0.477) = 0.217 for the year 1985; (0.706-0.515) = 0.191 for the year 1990; (0.729-0.545) = 0.184 for the year 1995; (0.747-0.577) = 0.170 for the year 2000; (0.755-0.611) = 0.144 for the latest year 2004 of the HD Report, 2006. Indian Human Development in contrast to Sri Lanka revealed India's performance in terms of human development initially in the year 1975 was wide in gap, which started declining during the last 19 years, i.e. 1990 to 2004 years.

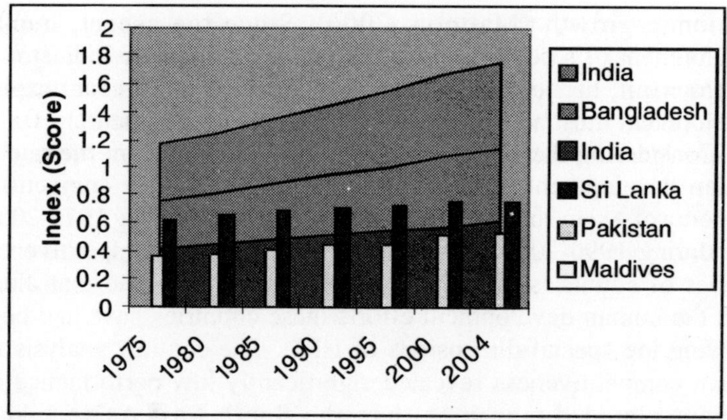

Fig. 11.5: Human Development Performance and Growth (In South Asia)

HRD for Human Development

Human development goes beyond the standard notion of economic development that has come to be synonymous with growth in real per capita income. It includes dimensions such as knowledge and longevity that reflect non-material aspects of the quality of life. However, the economic growth on non-material aspects (in terms of resource-based concept) cannot determine the knowledge and longevity the non-material aspects of the quality of life. It is comprehensible that unless there are sufficient jobs the non-material aspects of life cannot be ensured. Human development is dependent on total factor productivity of macro as well as micro economy. In the work of Dahlman, Carl and Utz., Anuja (2005) Total Factor Productivity (TFP) is taken to be a proxy for a nation's learning capability. Embarking on a new growth path of India, they commented that India has a rich choice set in determining its future growth path. The World Bank report by the authors stated on what India can achieve by the year 2020, based on different assumptions about its ability to use knowledge, even without any increase in the investment rate. While Goldman Sachs anticipates India to become the world's second largest economy after China, it counsels for great investments in its human capital for this prosperity to be equitable (Bana, 2007). Countless observers have suggested that the role of higher education in a knowledge-driven economy has never been more crucial as innovation and human capital which are seen as keys to future economic growth (Mattoon, 2006). Since the aspect, human development of a country is considered as an alternate indicator of development, henceforth, it is to be concluded that human capital development must also be crucial for human development.

Considering the pace of Indian human development the rate of human development is slower than the rate of highly competitive economy of Asian sub-region (Annual growth rate during 1975-2004, rate during 1990-2004 in Appendix Table 1). The competitiveness indices of countries of Asian sub-regions also indicate that along with the human development efforts these countries have/had been showing the special dimensions of HRD. The contrast analysis on Indian competitiveness revealed significantly low performance on human related dimensions than the South East Asian highly competitive nations. These dimensions are—Institutions, Health and Primary Education, Higher Education and Training, Market Efficiencies, Technological Readiness, Business Sophistication, and Innovation. The rate of Indian human development and competitiveness on these dimensions are revealing proportionately mismatch trend of development. India has to look after the aspect of human development, along with the poverty reduction and job creation. Again, it is difficult to depend on human development for its role on end of poverty, unless poor people walk for the hunt of job by realizing his ability and capability. Unless the poor people continue to apply their ability and capability, they will not be able to reduce their starvation. Jobless growth cannot help in sustaining human development for a long time. To sustain growth in Human Development for the longer time along with the competitive drive has to encompass the HRD efforts. Countless literature suggest on human development along with human resource development.

The logic behind the incorporation of HRD can be put in original conceptual frame of Global Competitiveness, and its indicators. But, by considering the knowledge, service revolution and competitiveness India along with original model of competition and development have to encompass more efficiency driven innovation. Unless proper emphasis is given to innovation and efficiency drive, sustainable human development cannot be achieved. To initiate sustainable human development along with the aim to keep pace with competitiveness the following two figures (Figs. 11.6, 11.7) would help understanding how human resource development would work as back ground for the human development along with a competitive drive.

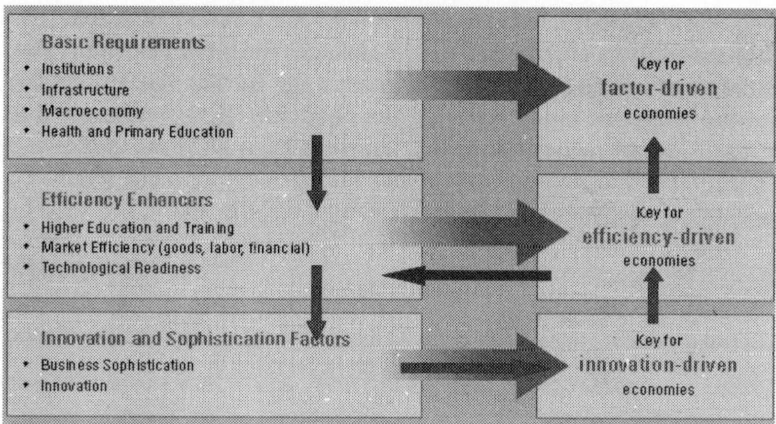

Fig. 11.6

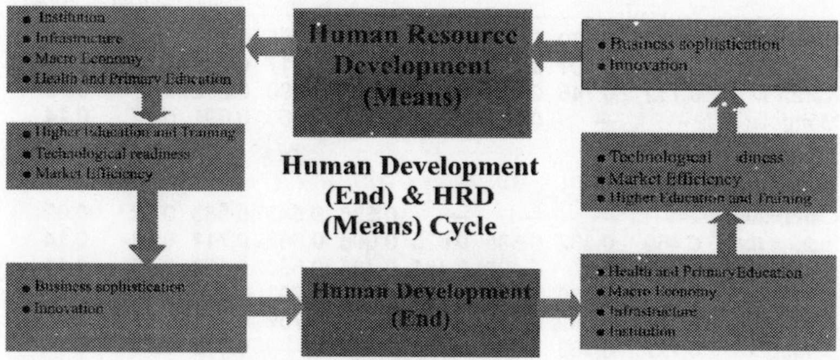

Fig.11.7

Implications and Conclusion

The study was primarily aimed to describe human resource development for sustainable human development with the available data of sub-region of Asia. It was thought the data available with author would be sufficient to justify the title of the paper. While in writing, the author felt the data insufficiency for triangulation, and in delving deep the emerging dimensions at time of articulation.

Hence, the study concentrated on the macro level HRD without the support of much data and references. However, the thought that emerged from the study would have wide implications for policy formulation for human development in the context of India. The contrast analysis and the test for the linkages to Human Development and Poverty would serve as background for further study. Last but not the least, the study revealed the need for HRD for sustainable human development and by emphasizing human resource development, more and sustainable human development would be possible as suggested by the HRD and HD Cycle.

APPENDIX

Appendix Table 1: Human Development Trend Human Development index (Score)

Groups	*1975*	*1980*	*1985*	*1990*	*1995*	*2000*	*2004*	*Annual growth Rate*	*Annual Growth Rate*
East Asia								*(1975-2004)*	*(1990-2004)*
China (PR)	0.527	0.560	0.569	0.628	0.685	0.785	0.768	0.13	0.15
Hong Kong	0.761	0.801	0.829	0.864	0.863	0.917	0.927	0.18	0.19
Korea ®	0.712	0.746	0.786	0.923	0.863	0.890	0.912	0.17	0.19
Mongolia	—	—	0.642	0.646	0.634	0.669	0.691	0.13	0.14
South East Asia									
Cambodia	—	—	—	—	0.536	0.545	0.583	0.12	0.09
Indonesia	0.469	0.532	0.585	0.626	0.665	0.682	0.711	0.13	0.14
Lao PDR	—	—	0.425	0.451	0.488	0.523	0.553	0.10	0.11
Malaysia	0.616	0.659	0.696	0.723	0.761	0.791	0.805	0.15	0.16
Philippines	0.655	0.689	0.695	0.722	0.738	0.759	0.763	0.15	0.16
Singapore	0.727	0.763	0.786	0.823	0.862	—	0.916	0.14	0.14
Thailand	0.615	0.664	0.680	0.717	0.751	0.775	0.784	0.15	0.16
Vietnam	—	—	—	0.618	0.661	0.696	0.709	0.14	0.14
South Asia									
Bangladesh	0.347	0.366	0.391	0.422	0.454	0.510	0.530	0.09	0.10
India	o.413	0.439	0.477	0.515	0.548	0.577	0.611	0.11	0.12
Maldives	—	—	—	—	—	—	—		
Pakistan	0.365	0.383	0.420	0.463	0.449	0.511	0.539	0.09	0.10
Sri Lanka	0.612	0.653	0.684	0.706	0.729	0.747	0.755	0.14	0.15
Mean	*0.5824*	*0.605*	*0.619*	*0.657*	*0.668*	*0.692*	*0.722*	*0.13*	*0.14*
Std. Dev	*0.140*	*0.148*	*0.146*	*0.150*	*0.141*	*0.134*	*0.133*		

REFERENCES

Aga, Anu (2006): On What Will it Take to Increase The Number of Women in Work Force? *Business Today*, Vol. 15, No. 1, January 15, 2006, pp. 196-206.

Bana, Sarus (2007): Reaching Higher; *Business India*, March-11, 2007, pp. 50-52.

Basu, Kaushik (2007): Let the Cream Percolate: Growth Gains The Meaning Only With More Job, Less Leakage of Funds, *Outlook* (*Special Issue*). 9th April, 2007, p. 26.

Birla, Kumar Mangalam (2006): On What will it to make India an Economic Superpower, *Business Today*, Vol. 15, No. 1, January 15, 2006, pp. 36-40.

Cho, Ahyoung (Chun) (2007): Gentle Power to Change the World, NIAS nytt, *Asia Insight*, No 3, 2007, July, pp. 7-9.

Dahlman, Carl and Utz., Anuja, (2005). *India and the Knowledge Economy Leveraging Strengths and Opportunities*, WBI Development Research Institute; (April 2005), World Bank.

Dutta, Saikat, Raman, Anuratha., and Mukerjee Arindam (2007). State of the Nation—Jobless Growth: A Ten Foot Trench, *Outlook* (*Special Issue*), 9th April, 2007, pp. 54-56.

Gobindarajan, Vijay (2006): On What will it Take for India to Become a Nation of Innovators? *Business Today*, Vol. 15, No. 1, January 15, 2006, pp. 160-184.

Hagel, John, Brown, John Seely (2006): Globalization & Innovation: Some Contrarian Perspective: Report Prepared for the Annual Meetinng of World Economic Forum in Davos, Switzerland; January 25-30, 2006, at *www.johnhagel.com;* www.johnseelybrown.com; www.edgepersonperspective.com

Huang, Yasheng and Khanna, Tarun (2003). *Can India Overcome China, Foreign Policy*, July-August 2003; at *www.foreignpolicy.com*

Hudock, Ann (2005): Laying the Foundation for Sustainable Development: Good Governance and the Poverty Reduction Strategy Paper; WORLD LEARNING Projects in International Development and Training 1015-15th Street NW, Suite 750 Washington, DC, *www.worldlearning.org*

Kumar, Rajib and Chadee, Doren (2002): International Competitiveness of Asian Firm: An Analytical Framework, ERD Working Paper No. 4, Asian Development Bank.

Lahiri, Ashok (2007): Deliverance from Deprivation, Reform have to chase expenses see if they are producing results; *Outlook* (*Special Issue*), 9th April, 2007, p. 26.

Lauridsen, Laurids S., Nordhaug, Kristen and *et al.* (February 2005): Glob Asia—Asia between global and regional challenges; A Research Framework for the 'Glob Asia Research Group' IDS Roskilde University, Denmank, Email: GLOBASIA@RUC.DK; *www.Globasia.DK*

Mattoon. Richard H. (2006): Can higher education foster economic growth?

Chicago Fed Letter (Essay). The Federal Reserve Bank of Chicago, August 2006, Number 229.

McCulloch, Douglas (2004): A Response to Frank Rotering's "Human Economics: A Theory for Humanity and the Environment", *Fiesta Review*, Commentaries on Human Economics.

Moore, Quinn and Schmidt Lucie (2004): Do Maternal Investments in Human Capital Affect Children's Academic Achievement? pp. 1-55, National Science Foundation, Corresponding Author: Lucie Schmidt, Department of Economics, Fernald House, Williams College, Williamstown, MA 01267; *lschmidt@williams.edu*.

Murthy, N.R. Narayan (2006): On What will it Take to rid India of Corruption? *Business Today*, Vol. 15, No. 1, January 15, 2006, pp. 212-215.

Nadar, Shiva (2006): On What will it take India to Bridge Digital Divide? *Business Today*, Vol. 15, No. 1, January 15, 2006, pp. 142-150.

Nilekani, M. Nandini (2006): On What Will it Take to Make Our Cities Truly World Class, *Business Today*, Vol. 15, No. 1, January 15, 2006, pp. 72-76.

Origin of the Crisis, Asia and the Global Crisis: Industrial Dimensions; Organization for Economic Co-Operation, OECD Report-2002.

Pachauri, R. K. (2006): On What Will it Take to Ensure Clean Water for All ? *Business Today*, Vol. 15, No. 1, January 15, 2006, pp. 84-86.

Poddar, Toshar, and Yi, Eva (January 22, 2007): India's Rising Growth Potential, Global Economics Paper No. 152, Economic Research from the GS Institutional Portal, at *https://portal.gs.com*

Premji, Azim (2006): On What will take to Achieve Universal Quality of Education? *Business Today*, Vol. 15, No. 1, January 15, 2006, pp.150-160.

Radjou, Navi (2006): How India, China Redefine the Tech World Order; The Innovation Edge—Meeting The Global Competitive Challenge, *Bay Area Economic Forum*, September 2006, pp. 20-25.

Shaw, Kiran Mazumder (2006). What it take to Ensure Health Care for All? *Business Today*, Vol. 15, No. 1, January 15, 2006, pp. 106-114.

Reports

Asia Pacific Human Development Report 2006, UNDP, pp. 29-48.

Global Competitiveness Report, 2007.

Hagel, John, Brown, John Seely. (2006). Globalization & Innovation: Some Contrarian Perspective: Report Prepared for the Annual Meetinng of World Economic Forum in Davos, Switzerland, January, 25-30, 2006, at *www.johnhagel.com; www.Johnseelybrown.com; www.edgepersonperspective.com*

Human Development Report, 2002.

Human Development Report, 2005.

Human Development Report, 2006.

India and the Knowledge Economy Leveraging Strengths and Opportunities,

WBI Development Research Institute; (April 2005). World Bank.

India's New Opportunities—2020: Report of the High Level Strategic Group, All India Management Association, "Management House"; The Boston Consulting Group; Confederation of Indian Industry.

Part-3 of *Asian Development Outlook* 2007.

Report of the Committee on India Vision 2020 *Chairman* **Dr. S. P. Gupta,** Planning Commission Government of India, New Delhi December, 2002.

Section Five

Human Development and Human Values

12

Gandhi, Gandhians and Thoughts on Indian Development: Random Reflections on Human Development

AMIYA P. SEN

> "Modern Societies aim at protecting economic rights while leaving economic functions except in moments of abnormal emergency to fulfil themselves. The motive which gives colour and quality public institutions, to their policy and economic thought is not the attempt to secure the fulfilment of tasks undertaken for the public service but to increase the opportunities open to individuals of attaining the objectives which they conceive to be advantageous to themselves."
>
> —R.H. Tawney (1921)

Even as I put together my thoughts for this paper it occurs to me that today, any one contributing to the debate on development speaks under the shadow of a great paradox. In contemporary India, one stares at both paucity and the problem of plenty, at stark deprivation and soaring dividends, at painful self-extinction and pompous self-indulgence. At least the more sensitive among us, I trust, have come to realize how, as Dickens once put it in the opening lines of one his novels, societies at some point of time, simultaneously manifest the best and the worst of human experiences. Perhaps it is flattering that today, Indians are listed among the world's richest individuals. Tragically though, this occurs amidst news of farmers consuming pesticide in order to escape the crippling burden of debts, of tribes being driven out of their traditional habitat to make way for some ill-conceived official project and of children dying by thousands out of sheer hunger and malnutrition. There is, on the one hand, our burgeoning middle class that happily foists the banner of '*India Shining*'. However, it is not less apparent to us that over three quarters of the Indian population cannot afford to spend even Rs. 20 a day on themselves and their families. Surveys for 2004-05 conducted by N.E.C.U.S reveal that nearly 80 per cent of this number belong to the unorganized sector and are socially identifiable as Muslims, Dalits and members of other depressed castes or classes. Some months back, there was exciting news of an Indian cricketer being awarded a sum of Rs. 1 crore for lifting the cricket ball out of the boundary ropes six times in succession. This happened to be cricketer whose annual income from match fees and sponsorships, so far as I could make out, probably exceeded a crore anyway. I have no moral authority to question the wisdom and generosity of the organization or individuals that decided to so reward the cricketer nor ask just how the awardee decided to spend the prize-money. On the other hand, I would have been immensely gratified to hear that this money was spent in a manner, relatively less affluent individuals chose to do. Jason Lepcha, who was officially rewarded for helping the Police apprehend the murderer of Hannah Claire Foster, spent all his award-money in setting up a free primary school at Dhotrey Tea Gardens, Darjeeling. This, as it then appeared to me, was plowing back into the soil what one took off it, to give back to the community what an individual owed it for his growth and upbringing. Lest I be taken to be a cynic and killjoy, let me confess that personally, I have nothing against extraordinary feats being suitably rewarded. What I fear though is a palpable displacement of our moral values, the weakening of our social conscience, the waning of responsible citizenship.

That development has to put up a human face and be backed by demonstrable popular will is an argument that has now gained considerable currency, especially with the launching of major state-sponsored projects. Not surprisingly, this has produced sharp debates and differences, at times, even violence. Perhaps more violence is in store as battle-lines are drawn every afresh. State agencies are now beginning to stake both their ideological position and political mandates on the strength and sustainability of their projects while dissenters and critics look to air more sophisticated counter-arguments and devise newer forms of protest. At Khejuri and Nandigram (both in West Bengal), 'development' had to be defended through the use of lethal bullets with or without the connivance of the State Administration. Opposition parties on the other hand, sensing a political kill have repeatedly brought public life to a halt, not caring to ponder at just how, daily wage-earners, hawkers or petty shop-keepers might meet the pressing needs of livelihood. As an ordinary citizen, I have often been acutely uncomfortable with the fact something that was started in the name of human development should also claim human lives.

II

As a historian, I am also persuaded to argue that the substance of the debate on development now raging in India has been significantly anticipated by some of our leading thinkers. This paper focuses on Gandhi and after him, a leading Gandhian thinker, J.C. Kumarappa. However, I have, at places, also briefly hinted at relevant and comparable elements of thought from the life and work of Rabindranath Tagore. Though they otherwise differed sharply over certain issues, there is much in Gandhi and Tagore that also brings them together, especially with respect to their thinking on India's endemic socio-economic problems. In the first place, they were quick to realize that in the Indian context, human development essentially devolved upon a suitable overhauling of the rural economy and society inhabited by an overwhelmingly large number of Indians. No less importantly, they acknowledge the need to evolve alternative conceptions of modernity—one that would be less imitative of models and practices devised in the West. Modernity, in other words, could not be taken to follow a universally predetermined path. Rather they had to be based on a realistic assessment of just what would be intelligible to a people or what most effectively implemented. The Gandhian utopia of '*Ramrajya*', for instance, underscored the idea of constructively applying a social and ethical idiom with which people in the north Indian countryside were deeply familiar. In this Gandhi and Tagore were also palpably guided by traditional Indian perceptions of man and of productive human labour. It seems to me that they preferred the traditional Indian paradigm of '*purnatwa*' (fullness) to that of 'perfection', essentially derived from Western positivist thought. Arguably, this allowed them to emphasise a more rounded and holistic approach to man. In concrete terms, this meant that backwardness could not be measured in terms of physical well-being alone. No less important here was (to use a typically Gandhian expression) 'soul-force', —an intensely moral and spiritual vision of man which alone could provide meaning to his material development. Life, in this view, was more sacred than mere livelihood.

As is only too well-known, Gandhi's critique of contemporary notions of development was first expressed in his *Hind Swaraj* (1910). For Gandhi, this work never lost its relevance for even as late as 1940, he was to recommend it to Nehru. However, with time, Gandhi also drew upon sources that seemed to substantiate the essential thrust of his arguments. A good part of this no doubt came from the writings of Europeans themselves, John Ruskin and Leo Tolstoy, to cite two of the more familiar names. However, he was also enthused by Sir Henry Maine's romanticized account of village India (*Village Communities of the East and West*) and its later adaptations by Indians like Radhakamal Mukerjee (*The Foundations of Indian Economy*) and Radha Kumud Mukerjee (*Local Government in Ancient India*). To this he added his critique of utilitarianism which was both notoriously anti-tradition and reluctant to make qualitative judgements. Even allowing for the fact that Gandhi's economic thinking never acquired the status of a formal economic theory, there were a few things distinctive about it. For one, Gandhi tended to treat economics as a moral science, blending ethics into generally well accepted laws of economic functioning. While self-sufficiency was important to Gandhi, at the heart of his economic thought lay the concepts of bread-labour and *aparigraha* (non-possession). The first was clearly borrowed from Western thought and the latter from the Indian ethical tradition. For Gandhi it was important that a man lived by his honest labour but only to the point of general well being, not indulgent prosperity. The concept of *aparigraha* strongly discouraged a man's coveting someone else's assets or more generally, turning acquisitive.[1] This, he took to be a vital safeguard against avarice, cut-throat competition and the spirit of accumulation that was integral to the modern market-economy. Effectively, non-possession was for Gandhi the best guarantee of non-violence for it was an acquisitive society that bred or encouraged violence and all forms of inequity. However, Gandhi believed that violence did not always emanate in the rich and the powerful classes and used against the socially deprived or marginalized. It could also be wrecked upon the strong and the affluent by a suffering people acutely conscious of their social deprivation. Gandhi's social panacea, therefore, was to avoid at all costs, a situation potentially capable of producing class-war. On the contrary, it attempted to bring about class harmony and class-reconciliation. To an extent, this is also reflected in the contemporary policies and programmes of the Indian National Congress which attempted to bring together peasant-producers and landlords, irrespective of their apparently divergent class interests. The idea of class-harmony was spelt out in a sophisticated, albeit also more utopian fashion, in the concept of 'Trusteeship', the seeds of which may be found in William Godwin's well known work *Political Justice*. This was a premise that was to significantly alter Gandhian frames of reference and the ways in which he sought to understand the world. Thus, whereas for Gandhi, the term '*Antyodya*' might have been a more literal translation of Ruskin's *Unto The Last*, he chose to change this to '*Sarvodaya*' for, his vision of social and ethical upliftment included the upper classes as well. Here, it might be briefly refer to the subtle but significant differences in emphasis between Gandhi's vision of community development. In the community projects that he launched, first in his own private estates at Kaliganj and Patisar (now in Bangladesh) and thereafter at Surul-Sriniketan, Tagore maintained that the work was essentially to be entrusted to 'community leaders' by which he meant men elected by the community itself. *Prima facie*, this stands in some contrast to the Gandhian doctrine of Trusteeship wherein the 'Trustees' were not only rich and powerful but virtually self-appointed. Also, in their specific class-origins, Tagore's community leaders were expected to be from the educated strata, — a fact that reflects the grossly underdeveloped state of indigenous industry and industrialist in the province of Bengal. Gandhi's association, on the other hand, was with some of the leading industrial houses in upper India.

It would be quite misleading to suggest that Gandhi was opposed to modernity *per se*. In his time, this term could not have been brushed away as the category of 'class' cannot be in contemporary social science discourse. And surely, he was not in principle against machines for he had high praise for the Singer sewing machine which he took to be a marvelous invention, punctiliously consulted his watch and regularly travelled by Railways,—all of which were by-products of a modern industrial civilization. It would be safer to say that he was against the dehumanization brought on by thoughtless mechanization. Gandhi would have been aware of how the use of machines tended to take away the very soul of the worker, robbing him of the aesthetic joy of creation, how the concept of 'waste' was endemic to an industrial society but above all, of the traumatizing fact that under modern industrialization, a worker was reduced to a mere wage-earner whereby his labour did not belong to himself but to the individual or institution that he worked for. I imagine that at some point in the debate on development he would have wanted to say that traditional ways of life were always the victim of an unequal competition for they never really had the opportunity to demonstrate their efficiency or worthiness.

Even in Gandhi's life time, the individual who most effectively carried forward his ideas on Indian development was J.C. Kumarappa. Kumarappa was trained in public finance and accounting and gave up a successful professional career in the West after being won over by Gandhian ideas. His writings, technically more coherent and erudite provided the ammunition to many contemporaries, not excepting Gandhi himself, to push forth their critique of capitalist economy. Both Gandhi and Kumarappa held the view that quintessentially, India's problems were not political in nature but economic and that very generally speaking, a meaningful economic transformation of the vast Indian countryside had to precede political freedom. A large part of Kumarappa's own writings centred on the key questions of forest management, fodder supplies, building bio-mass reserves and the need to address the shortfall in food crops resulting from the switch over to more lucrative cash-crops. Not surprisingly, Kumarappa's rise within the Congress hierarchy was meteoric. He was Secretary to the All India Village Industries Association (AIVIA) between 1933-55, a member of the Nehru Committee (constituted in 1947-48) to help formulate a document on the economic policy of the Congress government in free India, a member of the Planning Commission and Chairman of the Agrarian Reforms Committee of the A.I.C.C. between 1948 and 1950.

Kumarappa's vision for a free and economically liberated India is summed up in his work *Why Village India?* (Wardha, 1936), in which he emphatically echoes two of Gandhi's persistent points of criticism against an industrial civilization. In the first place, he reiterates the idea that capitalistic production caused affected the physical and moral character of the masses. A related point here was that industrialization of the nature current in India would not provide gainful occupation to masses for a sustained length of time. In his view, consumer goods had to be produced through decentralized methods that would strike at the very basis of a standardized consumption pattern. Importantly, he identified the Indian woman as the main creator of demand and the man the supplier. This, he took to be consistent with the practices that India had traditionally followed and one that was culturally most compatible with the ideas and habits of the people. Kumarappa was equally critical of both capitalism and communism both of which he believed to be unnatural and based on various forms of violence. They belittled man and took away his dignity. Under capitalism, the individual was 'gun-fodder' and under communism, a mere 'cog-in-the wheel' of some gigantic machine. He was also sufficiently under the shadow of the Mahatma to nurture fairly romanticized notions about Indian village economy and the 'unchanging' values and visions of the Indic civilization. The West, in his opinion, lacked true democracy; its idyllic location was still in India's perennially present village republics which, when left to themselves, admirably generated and used up their own resources. The plight of India's hungry towns and villages somehow escaped both Gandhi and Kumarappa; neither of them seems to have realized that over time, South Asia and more so, India, was to have one of the biggest concentrations of urban population.

We may also detect in Kumarappa's writings a growing conservatism that probably took roots in his somewhat uncritical and romanticized notions about Indian society and culture. Kumarappa was known to defend the joint-family system and quite anachronistic views on the division of labour and though himself a pious Tamil Christian, was consistently on the side of the *varna* system, albeit in a somewhat reformulated form. In Kumarappa's formulation, *varna*/caste could be dissociated from the accident of birth but yoked to one's intrinsic temperament and motives. Going by his analogy, a electrician who selflessly pursued the academic possibilities of science was a Brahmin; one who employed science to the project of industrialization was a Kshatriya; he who dealt in electric supply with an eye on material gain was a Vaisya and the man who entered the Government Electric Supply Department in order to obtain personal economic security was a Sudra.[2] This system, in Kumarappa's perception allowed for functional planning as opposed to production planning. It was a system that encouraged economic activity that was consistent with some universally valid moral axioms or laws and not, man's myopic and momentarily defined needs. Not surprisingly, Kumarappa's ideas were quite effectively appropriated by

Brahmanists and the Hindu Right. His critics found him to be both anachronistic and utopian; some were even allege that both he and his mentor, Gandhi were anti-science and secretly pro-capitalism. A capitalist, as was sometimes argued, may well hide behind the rhetoric of Trusteeship. Contemporary Socialists like Jai Prakash Narayan were quick to point out that even Ramrajya was bound to have paupers!

Neither Gandhi nor Kumarappa were sufficiently impressed with the new economic experiments launched in Soviet Russia. In fact, the former is known to have once cajoled his protégé for not sufficiently criticizing Soviet models of socializing industries. This, again, offers some contrast to the enthusiasm that Rabindranath showed for the changes that he personally witnessed in Russia. On his visit to post-revolutionary Russia, Tagore was most impressed with the absence of the 'vulgar conceit of wealth; in his Bengali correspondence (*Russiar Chithi/Letters from Russia*)[3] the changes are described as being nothing short of '*pralay*' [a radical reordering of the world]. Admittedly, Tagore had little or no idea about the historical and ideological differences that separated the birth of cooperative movements under early European Socialism, and that in force in Soviet Russia in the 1930s. Also, hitherto his approach in matters of social or economic reform was that of an indulgent *pater familia* who directed, regulated and slow-paced change from above. As with Gandhism, this was a view that rejected not private property *per se* but the excessive individualism of its enjoyment. All the same, Tagore's was on the whole, a more accommodative view that also more clearly sided with the question of bringing appropriate technology to the task of ameliorating human conditions. One important matter that Gandhi and Gandhians also failed to adequately acknowledge was that, though at times arduous, attitudes could be most effectively changed for the better with the aid of economic tools.

For three to four decades after Gandhi, development was caught up in fierce ideological battles that somehow overlooked basic operative problems. Ideally, rational economic planning had to take cognizance of three prerequisites. Planners had to constantly remind themselves of their goals, now the starting point as well as the stages through which to attain a certain objective. Sudhir Sen, a man who was for long associated with Tagore's Sriniketan Rural Development Project and subsequently, the D.V.C, perceptively writes of the practically unproductive confusion of ideologies:

> "...The Socialist rests content with a pious declaration of the goal. He begins where
> One should end. The Charkhaite (Gandhian) in spite of his protestations to the contrary
> Plans for the maintenance of the status quo as his ideal, a subsistence level of income.
> He mistakes the starting point for the goal and ends where one should begin. The machinite
> has a better grasp of the goal but he does not realize the full implications of the starting point
> nor does he show the stages by which we would reach the objective. He treats as a road what
> can be but a long series of steps. He plans but only for plan-less industrialization."[4]

Let me, in conclusion, return to the point I made at the beginning of this paper, viz. the burden of individual moral responsibility in the task of identifying areas of human development and of its execution. Only a few days back, Doordarshan flashed the interesting news of how an Andhra woman who had hitherto lived by begging, had been elected Sarpanch by her village. It emerges that this woman (having failed to recall her true name let me call her Jagadamma) used to distribute among her co-inhabitants in the village all food that exceeded her own personal requirements. Apparently, she did not fear a bad day when she might go without alms, nor think of hoarding what she had in excess for some material gain. And life now seems to have sufficiently rewarded her for her faith and optimism. Did she continue begging after being so elected? I would be very keen to know. In any case Jagadamma's case is quite reminiscent of what Gandhi himself had to once say about the individual as the effective moral agent. The paradox here is that although one of the most successful mobilizers of mass movements, Gandhi ultimately fell back on the spark that he believed could be best ignited within the individual conscience alone. Let me therefore wind up my story with a quote from Pyarelal:

> "In his [Gandhi's] structure composed of innumerable villages, there will be ever widening,

never ascending circles. Life will not be a pyramid with the apex sustained by the bottom.
But it will be an oceanic circle whose centre will be the individual always ready to perish for the villages, the latter ready top perish for the circle of villages, till at last (all) becomes one life, composed of individuals, never aggressive in their arrogance but ever humble, sharing the majesty of the oceanic circle of which they are integral units."[5]

Did we not need more Jagadammas?

NOTES

1. There is a strong possibility that Gandhi derived such thoughts from the opening lines of the *Isha Upanishad* which he valued highly and took to be a text that best summed up the essence of Hinduism. Incidentally, the *Isha Upanishad* had been a motivating text also in the case of the Brahmo leader, Maharshi Devendranath Tagore, the father of Rabindranath.
2. Here it is only relevant to mention that upholding the four-fold *varna* system as against caste (*jati*) discrimination was a feature that can be found not only in Gandhi himself but also other leaders belonging to mainstream nationalist politics.
3. Several years after his visit, the British government in India had serious intentions of prescribing this work.
4. Sudhir Sen, *Conflict of Economic Ideologies in India. An attempt at Reconciliation* (1941) cited in the author's *Rabindranath Tagore on Rural Reconstruction and Community Development in India.* Visva-Bharati. Revised and Enlarged Edition, 1991: 45.
5. Pyarelal, *Mahatma Gandhi: The Last Phase.* Vol.11 Ahmedabad,1956: 380-81.

13

Human Development and Early Indians' Thoughts

PROJIT KUMAR PALIT

Introduction

The basic purpose of human development is to improve the quality of life and dignity of human beings. So, the objective of development is to create an enabling environment for people to enjoy long, healthy and creative lives. But in modern world, human beings are frustrated for lack of schooling and health care, inadequate economic opportunities, violation of political liberties, etc. It is true that economic development can, to a large extent, reduce these issues. So the common idea of human development is capacity building for healthy and happy living. Further, human development has a firm commitment to democracy, human rights, human dignity and deep respect to environment. It draws on the magnificence of human potentiality amidst the widespread experience of narrowly circumscribed lives. So human beings are the real capital of any nation. They are powerful means for income-generation and upgradation of quality of life in the family, organization or country.

Concept of human development is not a new approach in India.[1] The root of the present concept of human development can be found in early Indian thoughts also.

The Upanisadas and Human Development

In sixth century B.C. Indian spiritual leaders gave a beautiful definition of human development in the *Chhandogya Upanisad* (1.1.10)[2]:

Yadeva vidyaya karoti, sraddhaya, Upanisada, tadeva viryavattram bhavati.

Whatever is done with *vidya*, *sraddha*, and Upanisad, that alone becomes supremely efficient.

Chhandogya Upanisad, traced three values which help mankind to develop their efficiency. These values are *vidya*, *sraddha* and Upanisad. *Vidya* means science or knowledge. If you want to be efficient you must have some knowledge, but that is not enough. Mere knowledge of a subject does not make you efficient. Second value is *Sraddha*—faith, here it does not mean faith in a dogma or creed or strongly held opinion, but faith in oneself, the impulse from within: I can, I can and the conviction that the work you are doing is worthwhile and that there is a meaningfulness to life and to the world and also that faith extends to faith in other members of the work team. Shankaracharya also defines *Sraddha* as *astikyabuddhi*—the totality of positive attitudes. This faith and conviction increases all work-efficiency. The Upanisad considers that *Vidya* and *Sraddha* are not enough, that a third value also has to be added to the two in order to achieve supreme efficiency. This is Upanisad which is deep thinking, meditative thinking on the subject concerned. Any work that has behind these three values of *Vidya*, *Sraddha* and Upanisad alone becomes *Viryavattaram*, of superior energy. So superior efficiency will come when we combine with energy of knowledge the energies of these other two values. When all these three energies are combined, man get a type of human excellence which has the power to move the world[3].

All human developments, including the spiritual, lie hidden in the child. We want to help the child to bring out these enormous developments, says Kathaupanishad[4] in these words:

Esha sarveshu bhuteshu
Gudho atma na prakashate
Drishyate tvagryaya buddhya
Sukshmaya sukshmadarshibhih—

This (infinite) *Atman* is present in every being, but lies hidden and (therefore) is not manifest; but it can be realized by the subtle and penetrating reason of those who are trained to perceive subtler and subtler truths.

All human development is based upon the discovery of some or more of these profound possibilities hidden within every human child and of the methods and techniques adopted to bring them out. Behind those eyes of the child lurk energies and talents that will come out later as an Olympic champion, a great scientist, a wise statesman, a creative artist, or a great saint. But none of these possibilities can be detected or felt by our sensory system, or by our mind dependent on that system. They exist in a dimension beyond man's sensory verification, just like the possibilities of a big tree lying beyond our sensory grasp in the depth of its tiny seed where they remain hidden, 'coiled up' as India's *kundalini yoga* expresses it[5]. But they manifest steadily to our sensory verification from the first appearance of the sprout, and thereafter, as it grows into a large tree.

Human Development and Harmony of Indian Values

In history, the world had two great cultures in the ancient past, which have developed philosophies leading to distinct types of human excellence, distinct types of human greatness—one, the ancient Hindu, which has influenced most of Asia, and the other, the Ancient Greek, which has influenced the whole of the West. These two have made very distinctive contributions to human culture. Each of these two cultures has its own uniqueness. Whatever, was achieved by the Greeks, and later on by the Romans, is what we find, in an enlarged form, and with modern science added, in modern Western culture. Whatever, excellences we get in this Western culture is found assimilated in Swami Vivekananda, as he had assimilated the excellences of his own ancient and continuing Indian culture and tradition.[6] And he made a unique discovery, that no culture is perfect, each culture has specialized only in some values and neglected other values due to that very specialization, and all these separate world cultures are essentially aspects of one total human culture and are, therefore, complementary and not mutually exclusive. All this he did by the time he was 29 years of age when he came to America in 1893, started his great work in the West and in India, and passed away at the early age of 39. But within this short time, to achieve high character and excellence and to make an impact on the minds and attitudes of men and women in two subcontinents, was great work indeed.[7] In Indian history, we have the example of *Bhagavan Buddha* of the sixth century B.C., who attained enlightenment at the age of about 36, and travelled through many areas of north India and imparted his message to thousands till his death at the age of 80; and his teachings peacefully transformed, in the next few centuries, India and much of Asia[8]. Again, we have another such example in the eighth century A.D. and that was Shankaracharya. Just 32 years of human life; and within that short period, Shankaracharya shook up India intellectually and spiritually. And in the modern age, India produced this great teacher Swami Vivekananda.[9] What are those essential elements constituting human development within India and in her teaching? According to Swami Vivekananda, education is the manifestation of the perfection already in man. We can deal with this subject from two points of view. One, from the point of view of human character that one gets from a good education. It is understood that education is meant not only to give us knowledge and information but also to build up our character. William James and William McDougall, both had laid stress on the character-building component of all true education—physical health and well-being, depth of thought, strength of conviction, faith in oneself, the humanistic impulse, and practical efficiency; all these constitute one type of character-excellence, which, along with the virtue of moderation, is found upheld in Greek culture. William James has written many books, one of which—a thought provoking one, is: *Varieties of Religious Experience*. One of the books written by McDougall is titled *Character and the Conduct of Life*. Modern Western education gave this wonderful character-excellence to Swami Vivekananda. Through this he assimilated what he later on would designate as the Greek ideal of 'manliness'. The Greeks laid great stress on these values. Modern Western character types are essentially derived from this Greek and Roman ideal of manliness, along with some other values gathered in the course of history.[10] It is a type of education imparting character-strength to man to enable one to handle efficiently the world of man and nature around him or her. This is one aspect of education; but there is also another aspect of education, with greater stress on education of man in depth. These two aspects are highlighted in the post-war period by the UNESCO appointed Commission to investigate the nature of education humanity needs in the post-war period. That Commission was presided over by the French Minister of Education, who later on became French Prime Minister, namely, Eduard Faure. And that Commission submitted a report after investigating the subject of the current systems of education and the demands of the new human situation in the post-war period.

This report is in its interesting and meaningful title 'Learning to be' till now education has been essentially 'Learning to do'. But this Commission says what the earlier thinkers like William James and McDougall had upheld, that while retaining 'Learning to do', post-war education must add also 'Learning to be'. Thus a new dimension to education is added by that phrase to be, along with the current, phrase to do. It is true Modern Civilization is a highly technical. So the education must equip one with tremendous work-efficiency; and work-efficiency consists of knowledge and translation of knowledge into action.

Humanism and Western World

Concept of humanism has also originated in the past but divided in two parts—one west and other east. Western humanism traces its ancestry to the ancient Greeks and Romans. Greek humanism was limited to its own citizens and excluded the non-Greeks and the slaves from its blessings. Roman humanism was broader, but did not also extend to the slaves[11]. Both were secular and non-religious. Then came Christianity, preaching its own humanism, based on its narrow theology, first to the people of the Roman Empire and, later, to people of Europe as a whole. But this Christian humanism also was exclusive; it was limited to the believers in its own narrow creed and dogma; it did not extend only to non-Christians, but also to its own dissidents in creed and to all scientists and rationalists. Western humanism in general, and Christian humanism in particular, received their most serious shock from the very violent Thirty-Years' War between the Protestants and Catholics in Germany. Man killed man in the name of a common God and religion, reducing the population of Germany, according to historians, from 25 to 5 million. This was a traumatic experience for all thinking Europeans to shift their faith from God to man[12]. This shift of faith from god to man was helped by the European's discovery of Greek humanism, in the wake of its contact with the thought and culture and literature of classical Greece in the fifteenth and sixteenth centuries; this modern Western humanism, strengthened by physical sciences and technology, held out melioristic hopes of full human development in peace and plenty all over the world. It steadily gained strength and prestige for three hundred years, up to 1914.[13] Then came the devastating First World War, when Western man hated and killed brother Western man to an extent unprecedented in history. This was followed by continuous tensions of the post-war years, to culminate in the more devastating Second World War, with its additional Nazi brutalities and gruesome murder of millions of Jews. These traumatic experiences shook to the very foundations Western man's faith even in man, just as the Thirty-Years' War earlier had destroyed his faith in God. They shattered his faith even in humanism itself. The Second World War has left Western man with no focus of faith and loyalty either to a God above or man below, breeding in him a cynical attitude with respect to all values—religious and other-worldly, or human and this-worldly, for ethical and moral; and it has led him to opt for a plunge into a crude materialism and to bend his efficiency for the satisfaction of his organic cravings during the short span of his physical existence. This has, in turn, resulted in generating in him inner tensions, privations, and psychic distortions to an alarming degree. Into this Western human context came a new challenge, in the form of the Bolshevik Revolution and the hope of a new human civilization led by the USSR, promising peace and plenty round the world. After impressive achievements in the field of mass human developments during its first four decades, this new experiment also is showing severe inner tensions within the individual man and woman in the USSR, in the form of increase in crime, drunkenness, and other psychic distortions, and intense conflicts between one Marxist state and another. Marxist humanism goes far, but not far enough, to ensure human fulfilment. Vedanta helps Marxism to carry its study of man into the depth of the human spirit and to base its undoubtedly promising human experiment on the rock of the divine in man and not on the sands of his physical and organic system. The Greeko-Roman and modern Western people have achieved a type of human development based on this faith in oneself and the promethean spark it ignited in them. But with these they have built up a high level of social welfare and the spirit of human individuality and dignity. But Vivekananda pointed out to the people of the West that this did not exhaust the scope of human excellence, the scope of the science of human possibilities. So man is not only a member of social community or a political personality but there is also a higher dimension of human development and excellence. That is called the spiritual dimension of human growth and excellence. If the first one is a horizontal and lateral growth, this second one is a vertical and inward growth. Aristotle said that man is a social animal. This is true; we need that gregarious background for our own growth;

but man has a vertical dimension, which calls for a deepening of his awareness, for a spiritual growth within. This is a wonderful truth about man, says Vedanta; it is not a creed or a dogma but a veritable truth which has been realized by many sages in East and West and can be verified by all. Even in ancient Greek culture this higher dimension of excellence was placed before man in the famous dictum of the Oracle of Delphi: 'Man, know himself.' It is not enough that you know the external environment. There is a profound inner environment also to be investigated and realized.

There was only one great Greek who understood this truth and realized it; and that was Socrates. He realized himself as the infinite and immortal *Atman*; and the Greeks, who knew only the socio-political dimension of man, the horizontal dimension, could not understand him. It was something beyond their comprehension. They well knew man wrestling with forces outside, and establishing his hegemony over the external world. But the greatness of Socrates was something deep, something subtle. It is a great tragedy that the Athenian state could not appreciate the high spiritual dimension of Socrates; and therefore, he was condemned to death. He was described by the judges as a corrupter of the Athenian youth. What a sad description! And what human excellence and greatness! But the socio-political philosophy of the Greeks could not grasp that character excellence. This is not only the example of Socrates but also we refer to Jesus Christ. Jesus also gave tremendous message of man's spiritual inwardness. But the socio-political philosophy of the Jews of the time could not comprehend it and condemned him to death. Athenians and the Jews could understand and appreciate the excellence of the socio-political character; but not anything higher than that. That illustrates the truth of the remark of Bertrand Russell: If you teach people faster than they can learn, you are in for trouble!

Humanism of Vivekananda and Indian History

Vivekananda's programme of human development in his own country was thus designed to be achieved not in an isolated exclusive national context, but in the broadest context of international cooperation. He advocated internationalism and international cooperation long before that concept became an international reality[14]. Vivekananda pointed this out as one of the sweetest fruits of India's humanism. It is also illustrated by the spread of Buddhism throughout Asia in a uniformly peaceful manner. Humanism cannot coexist with any predatory attitude or behaviour; it cannot coexist also with any intolerant attitude and behaviour.

We may consider India's history from two points of view: firstly, its successes; secondly, its failures. It has failed in certain fields, but it has registered success in certain other fields. It has so far failed to evolve a truly egalitarian social order, as pointed out by Vivekananda in his writing referred to earlier; and it is treating this as its supreme national objective in this modern period of her long history. But it has succeeded in developing and maintaining a uniformly peaceful attitude and policy in its international and inter-religious relations. It is impressive that, during her long history of about five thousand years, India has never gone outside her boundaries to conquer and enslave and exploit other nations, even when she had the political and military power to do so. This is the sweet fruit of her philosophy of man in depth, of her vision of the One Self in all, which made her evaluate man as man, and not as conditioned by his external variable factors such as race, creed, or political nationality. Universal peace and toleration derives only from a universal vision.

Vivekananda's humanism is based on this universal Vedantic vision of man as the Atman. This vision of India's sages and philosophers did not remain as a vision, but was given unique political expressions by several Indian political states at the all-India as well as provincial levels, among whom the most outstanding example was the policy and programme of the Mauryan Emperor Ashoka of the third century before Christ[15]. Experiencing remorse after his successful but bloody war with his neighbouring Kalinga state, Ashoka renounced all wars as the instrument of state policy and, as proclaimed through his numerous rock and pillar edicts, many of which still exist, he silenced all war drums, *yuddha-bheri*, and struck the kettle-drums of truth and justice, *dharma-bheri*; and this not only in the political and international fields, but also in the fields of inter-religious relations[16]. This wise policy of non-violence, active toleration, and international understanding was taken up by his successors also at the all-India and provincial levels, who extended welcome and hospitality to successive foreign racial and religious groups, and refugees fleeing from persecution from their own countries, like the Jews and the early Christians from West Asia and the Zoroastrians from Iran. Today, the whole world is seeking for, is in need of, this kind of spiritual growth which releases that type of divine energy resource to match with, and to digest, the energy resources released by modern physical science and technology. The latter has annihilated physical distances between man and man remains to be solved. On the other hand, that mental distance is increasing, not diminishing, in spite of scientific knowledge and technical power. This is revealed in the ever-increasing violence, crime, and delinquency, even juvenile delinquency, in all parts of the world, and in the sex and drug explosions rocking modern society. Bertrand Russell felt the need for knowledge but he also gave the warning to modern man—"Knowledge is power, but it is power for evil as much as for good. It follows that, unless men increase in wisdom as much as in knowledge, increase of knowledge will be increase of sorrow."[17]

Conclusion

Modern man has better physical bodies and health in past ages and he is also immensely nourished mentally and intellectually compared to his predecessor. But we find modern man getting increasingly alienated both from himself and from others. He is unhappy, tense, peaceless, given often to inflicting violence on others or suicide on himself. Swami Vivekananda realized above tragic situation developing even in his time and he warned of its intensification in the decades ahead, and emphasized the need for modern civilization to change its direction from human sensuality to human spirituality. And he preached the philosophy of Vedantic humanism, with its vision of the infinite divine possibilities in man, and man's organic capacity to realize these in his life. This is wisdom, this is knowledge maturing into wisdom, that India developed in her ancient *Upanishads* and the *Bhagavad Gita*, and which got retested and re-authenticated in succeeding ages by Buddha, Shankaracharya, Sri Ramakrishna, Sri Chaitanya, and many other luminous sages, possessed of brilliant intellects and universal hearts. They never thought or taught in narrow terms of sects or creeds or races or nationalities. They saw man as man, saw his infinite divine possibilities, felt compassion for the tragedy of his creatureliness and unfulfilments. They thus became the bearers of a luminous philosophy of humanism, at once rational, universal, practical, and dynamic. And Vivekananda expounded that Vedantic humanism in India and in the West, in the context of modern thought and modern needs and he also gave the inspiring message about the human excellence—"Teach yourselves, teach everyone, his real nature; call upon the sleeping soul and see how it awakes. Power will come, glory will come, goodness will come, purity will come, and everything that is excellent will come, when this sleeping soul is roused to self-conscious activity".[18]

NOTES

1. Fukuda-parr Sakiko, Shiva Kumar, A.K (2003): *Readings in Human Development*, New York, pp. 1-7.
2. *Chhandogya Upanisad*, Puna, 1942, p. 10.
3. Swami Ranganathananda: Swami Vivekananda and Human Excellence, Harvard University Lecture, Kolkata, 1990, p. 17.
4. *Katha Upanishad*: Kolkata, 1993, p. 12.
5. Swami Ranganathananda: Swami Vivekananda his humanism, Kolkata, Moscow University Lecture, 2005, p. 13.
6. Swami Tapasyananda: "The Nationalistic and Religious Lectures of Swami Vivekananda, Kolkata, 1990, pp. 55-56
7. Swami Ranganathananda: Harvard University Lecture, *Op. cit.*, pp. 10-11.
8. Radhakrishnan, S.: *Gautam Buddha*, Bombay, 1949, pp. 56-58.
9. Swami Ranganathananda: Harvard University Lecture, *op. cit.*, p. 11.
10. Swami Tapasyananda: *op. cit.*, pp. 54-59.
11. Radhakrishnan, S.: *Eastern Religions and Western Thought*, 1969, London, O.U.P., pp 381-382.
12. Toynbee, Arnold: *An Historian's Approach to Religion*, pp 180-200.
13. Khurana, K.L.: *Modern Europe*, Agra, 1998, p. 135.
14. Swami Ranganathananda: Moscow University Lecture, *op. cit.* p. 56.
15. Basham, A.L. (ed): *Cultural History of India*, Oxford, 1983, p. 39.
16. *Ibid.*, p. 42.
17. Russell, Bertrand: *Impact of Science on Society*, New York, 1953, pp. 120-121.
18. The complete works of Swami Vivekananda, Vol. 3, 1960, p. 193.

14

Right to Work: A Constitutional Contour and its Human Development Perspective

PARTHA PRATIM PAUL

Significance of Right to Work

Why right to work is so important for Human Development:

(a) It is for survival of human beings. Survival is the primary instinct or basic necessity of human beings, for which the role of right to work is extremely crucial.

(b) It is for the decent living of human beings. There are some basic and bare necessities of life to live in a civilized society, which is possible only through right to work.

(c) It is to maintain standard of living of human beings in a meaningful way. Life means quality of life as understood in its richness rather than mere animal existence of life in the world. So to add qualitative value to life, right to work is essential.

(d) It is for all-round development of man—emotional, physical, intellectual, social, moral and economic.

(e) Other valuable rights of human beings solely depend on this for their effective realization—right to education, right to dignity, right to environment, right to livelihood, right to equality, right to freedom all of which are the various indicators of human development. Without right to work, these rights would be meaningless.

(f) It is also important to bring about a truly egalitarian social order in the society through Rule of Law.

No discussion is required to explain how much important this right is. If this right is guaranteed as an affirmative action, achieving the goals of human development would be a much easier task. It would bring back smiles in the faces of billions and billions of people. It would definitely wipe out the tears from the eyes of billions and billions of people of this country. The state has a very important role as well as responsibility in ensuring every person the right to work. The state through the legal machinery can surely take steps to ensure that such rights are guaranteed to every human being since every man has a right to lead a dignified life free from the fear of economic, social, emotional and political deprivation.

Conceptual Framework of Right to Work

There may be various meanings of right to work. But conceptually, right to work means right to employment for all in the country. It is in the form of an obligation of the state, one kind of affirmative action or commitment to provide with employment according to the capabilities and efficiencies of those people, especially of those people who are not getting employment at all or not getting what actually they deserve. It also can be in the nature of an assurance from the state not to deny this right when people are in employment in different sectors of the economy. In this backdrop it is very much essential to know the nature and characteristics of this right to work, i.e. right to employment in the constitutional framework of India. It is also very much pertinent to know what steps must be taken to make this most valuable right accessible to each and every person of this country.

Objectives of Fundamental Rights

"They were included in the Constitution in the hope and expectation that one day the tree of true liberty would bloom in India."[1]

"These fundamental rights represent the basic values cherished by the people of this country since Vedic times and they are calculated to protect the dignity of the individual and create conditions in which every human being can develop his personality to the fullest extent. They weave a pattern of guarantees on the basic structure of human beings and impose negative obligations of the state not to encroach on individual liberty in its various dimensions. It is apparent from the enunciation of these rights that the respect for the individual and his capacity for individual violation which finds expression, there is not a self-fulfilling prophecy. Its purpose is to help the individual to find his own liability, to give expression to his creativity and to prevent governmental and other forces from alienating the individual from his creative impulses."[2]

"When the constitution makers enacted Part III dealing with fundamental rights, they inscribed in the Constitution certain basic rights which inhere in every human being and which are essential for enfoldment and development of his full personality. These rights represent the basic values of a civilized society and the constitution makers declared that they shall be given a place of pride in the Constitution and elevated to the status of fundamental rights. The long years of the freedom struggle inspired by the dynamic spiritualism of Mahatma Gandhi and in fact the entire cultural and spiritual history of India, formed the background against which these rights were enacted and consequently, these rights were conceived by the constitution makers not in narrow limited sense but in their widest sweep, for the aim and objective was to build a new social order where man will not be mere plaything in the hands of the state or a few privileged persons but there will be full scope and opportunity for him to achieve the maximum development of his personality and the dignity of the individual will be fully assured. The constitution makers recognized the spiritual dimension of man and they were conscious that he is an embodiment of divinity, what the great Upanishad verse describes as "the children of immortality" and his mission of life is to realize the ultimate truth. This obviously he cannot achieve unless he has certain basic freedoms..."[3]

Fundamental rights are enforceable against the state if state violates fundamental rights of the people of India.

The Nature and Characteristics of Right to Work, i.e. Right to Employment in the Constitutional Framework of India

There are some named fundamental rights in the Constitution of India i.e. right to equality, right to freedom, right to life and liberty, right to religion, right to get constitutional remedy, etc. But there is no such named fundamental right like right to work, i.e. right to employment.

It does not find place in any express provision of Constitution of India. Now the question is "though the right to work, i.e. right to employment is not a named fundamental right, can it be an inalienable part of a named fundamental right?"

When a Right Though Not a Named Fundamental Right, can be a Fundamental Right by Becoming Part of Fundamrental Right

Interpretation of Article 21—right to personal liberty, Constitution of India, is very much encouraging. "The expression personal liberty in Article 21 is of widest amplitude and it covers a variety of rights, which go to constitute the personality of man." As a result of this liberal interpretation of right to personal liberty, it was declared by Hon'ble Supreme Court in famous *Maneka Gandhi case* that right to personal liberty under Article 21, Constitution of India took within its sweep right to go to foreign countries, though right to go abroad was not a named fundamental right as such. This is equally and fairly true about right to life as well under Article 21.

The rationale or justification is that "Even if a right is not specifically named, it may still be a fundamental right, if it is an integral part of a named fundamental right or partakes of the same basic nature and character as that fundamental right."[4] According to this line of thinking right to work, i.e. right to employment must be integral part of right to life or partakes of the same basic nature and character of right to life.

Article 21 of the Constitution also assures right to life. Influencing by this judgement to make right to life meaningful and effective, Supreme Court put up expansive interpretation and brought within its ambit right to education, health, environment, dignity, livelihood, etc. as fundamental rights. Because life means quality of life as understood in its richness which definitely includes right to work, i.e. right to employment. Moreover, life in Article 21 does not connote mere animal existence of continued drudgery through life. Hence, there is no justification to bring right to work within the ambit of right to life, under Article 21.

Supreme Court of India on Right to Work

Delhi Transport Corporation Case

"The right to life includes right to livelihood. The right to livelihood, therefore, cannot hang on to the fancies of individuals in authority.

The employment is not a bounty from them, nor can its survival be at their mercy. Income is the foundation of many fundamental rights and when work is the only source of income, the right to work becomes as much fundamental as right to life. Fundamental rights can ill afford to be consigned to the limbo of undefined premises and uncertain applications. That will be a mockery to them. Both the society and the individual employees, therefore, have an anxious interest in service conditions being well defined and explicit to the extent possible. The arbitrary rules, which are also sometimes described as Henry VIII Rules, can have no place in any service conditions." Law as a social engineering requires to remove the existing imbalances and to further the progress serving the needs of Socialist Democratic Republic under the rule of law. Prevailing social conditions and actualities of the life are to be taken into account to adjudge the dispute and to see whether the interpretation would subserve the purpose of the society. The arbitrary, unbridled and naked power of wide discretion to dismiss a permanent employee without any guideline or procedure would tend to defeat the Constitutional purpose of equality and allied purposes."[5]

Air India Statutory Corporation Case

"It would be seen that all essential facilities and opportunities to the poor people are fundamental means to development, to live with minimum comforts, food, shelter, clothing and health. Due to economic constraints, though right to work was not declared as fundamental right, right to work of workman, lower class, a middle class and poor people is means to development and source to earn livelihood. Though right to employment cannot as a right be claimed but after the appointment to a post or an office, be it under the state, its agency, instrumentality, juristic person or private entrepreneur it is required to be dealt with as per public element and to act in public interest assuring equality, which is a genus to Article 14 and all other concomitant rights emanating there from are species to make their right to life and dignity of person real and meaningful." "When its correctness was doubted and its reference to the Constitution Bench was made in '*Delhi Transport Corporation Case*', while holding that Delhi Road Transport Authority was an instrumentality of state, it was held the employment is not a bounty from the state nor can its survival be at their mercy. Income is the foundation of many fundamental rights and when work is the soul source of income. The right to work becomes as much fundamental as right to life. Law as a social machinery requires to remove the existing imbalances and to further the progress serving the needs of Socialist Democratic Republic under the rule of law. Prevailing social conditions and actualities of the life are to be taken into account to adjudge the dispute and to see whether the interpretation would subserve the purpose of the society."[6]

High Court of Bombay

Shobha Vitthal Kolte Case

"In '*Air India Statutory Corporation Case*', it is noted that Article 41 provides that state shall within the limits of its economic capacity and development; make effective provisions for securing the right to work, to education and to public assistance in case of unemployment, old age, sickness and disablement and in other cases of undeserved want. In other words, the right to employment in the absence of suitable legislation cannot be placed on the same footing as right to livelihood. Though, it appears that apex court has observed the right to work becomes as much fundamental as right to life that would be once a person is appointed.

When its correctness was doubted and its reference to the Constitution Bench was made in '*Delhi Transport Corporation Case*', while holding that Delhi Road Transport Authority was an instrumentality of state, it was held that employment is not a bounty from the state nor can its survival be at their mercy. Income is the foundation of many fundamental rights and when work is the soul source of income, the right to work becomes as much fundamental as right to life. Law as a social machinery requires to remove the existing imbalances and to further the progress serving the needs of Socialist Democratic Republic under the rule of law. Prevailing social conditions and actualities of the life are to be taken into account to adjudge the dispute and to see whether the interpretation would subserve the purpose of the society.

"This observation must be considered in tune what is set out in the judgement. So reading, it would mean that the right to work as fundamental right can be considered as fundamental right in those cases where there is a legislative guarantee in the form of legislation. In the absence of right to work being fundamental right, it would not fall within expression life under Article 21 and if so would not fall within the definition of Human Rights as set out under Section 2(d) of the Act."[7]

Conclusion

Present Scenerio

Right to work for everyone in this country is a long cherished dream. But it has become a distant dream indeed. The dream is shattered and frustrated simply due to non-availability of right to work, i.e. right to employment. It is not known how many people are not getting basic and bare necessities of their lives. It is also not known how many people are not in a position to maintain minimum or decent standard of living. It is also not known how many people are failing to develop their talents and potentialities for the welfare of the society—resulting in wastage of human resources. Life has become a matter of liability, burdensome rather than a matter to celebrate and rejoice. Due to lack of right to work, i.e. right to employment, life has become full of miseries and anxieties to those people who are not getting. It is, therefore, only too evident that the basic tenets of the goals of attaining human development are seriously impaired. Such issues also have long-term implications which not only the common man but even the state machinery has to be extremely careful about. If the people themselves are not able to maintain the basic essentials of a minimum quality of life and provide basic education and health care facilities for their family members the duty and obligations of the state becomes perennial and permanent. For such purposes unproductive spending on social sector services becomes a compulsion for the state. Development under such a situation can never become sustainable.

Analysis of the Judgements—Little Done, Vast Undone

Truly the nature of right to work, i.e. right to employment is fundamental. It is an integral part of right to life and partakes of the same basic nature and character of right to life. But it is like this in the context of when someone is already in employment. When a person already is in work, State cannot deprive him of his right except the procedure established by law, which is fair, good, just and reasonable according to Article 21.

There is no such obligation on the part of the state to provide with right to work, i.e. right to employment to the people who deserve. It does not mandate the state with the obligation to take affirmative actions for the full realization of the fundamental right, until and unless there is legislation. But there is no such barrier on the state not to take affirmative actions for full realization of fundamental rights, i.e. right to work.

Recently there is one welcome step as because of legislation, i.e. National Rural Employment Guarantee Act. There is a ray of hope in the minds of the people as the State has taken some affirmative actions to guarantee employments (manual labours) where the people from below the poverty line can get employment for some months.

It is really appreciable that the judiciary has come a long way by interpreting Article 21, Constitution of India—right to life and personal liberty but suddenly stopped at a point short of including right to work, i.e. right to employment as a facet of right to life in the form of an obligation to provide work. Until and unless, judiciary shows courage and takes it as a challenge towards including right to work, i.e. right to employment as fundamental right everything would be a futile exercise. Otherwise State, will continue with this deceiving economic policy which would not be creating employment opportunities for all, especially to those who deserve.

Recommendations

Against this backdrop, for the full realization of right to work, i.e. right to employment to make the dream a reality:

(a) The meaning of deprivation must be extended so that even if the state does not ensure and guarantee right to work, i.e. right to employment of those who actually deserve, it would be a clear deprivation except the procedure established by law, which is not fair, good, just and reasonable.
(b) The National Rural Employment Guarantee Act is very limited in its scope. This Act has a long way to go to cover those people who deserve work. It must also be widened, though which unemployed persons would get employments according to their qualifications, knowledge, ability and efficiency, remains an issue to be resolved.

In the words of Justice Field of United States in no uncertain terms it can be said that "By the term 'LIFE', something more is meant than mere animal existence. The inhibition against its deprivation extends to all those limbs and facilities by which life is enjoyed."

Granville Austin as referred in *Maneka Gandhi* vs. *Union of India*, AIR 1978 SC.

NOTES

1. P.N. Bhagwati, J in *Maneka Gandhi* vs. *Union of India*, AIR 1978 SC.
2. P.N. Bhagwati, J in *Maneka Gandhi* vs. *Union of India*, AIR 1978 SC.
3. *Maneka Gandhi* vs. *Union of India*, AIR 1978 SC.
4. *Delhi Transport Corporation* vs. *Delhi Transport Corporation, Majdoor Union*, AIR 1991 SC 101.
5. *Air India Statutory Corporation* vs. *United Labour Union*, AIR 1997 SC 645.
6. *State of Maharashtra* vs. *Shobha Vittal Kolte*, AIR 2008 Bom 44.
7. *Munn* vs. *Illinois*, (1887) 94 U.S. 113.

Index